Promising Practices
in Supporting Success
for Indigenous Students

This work is published under the responsibility of the Secretary-General of the OECD. The opinions expressed and arguments employed herein do not necessarily reflect the official views of OECD member countries.

This document and any map included herein are without prejudice to the status of or sovereignty over any territory, to the delimitation of international frontiers and boundaries and to the name of any territory, city or area.

Please cite this publication as:
OECD (2017), *Promising Practices in Supporting Success for Indigenous Students*, OECD Publishing, Paris.
http://dx.doi.org/10.1787/9789264279421-en

ISBN 978-92-64-27941-4 (print)
ISBN 978-92-64-27942-1 (PDF)

The statistical data for Israel are supplied by and under the responsibility of the relevant Israeli authorities. The use of such data by the OECD is without prejudice to the status of the Golan Heights, East Jerusalem and Israeli settlements in the West Bank under the terms of international law.

Foreword

Following the International Summit on the Teaching Profession, hosted by Alberta (Canada) in 2015, Alberta Education initiated this collaborative project to improve learning outcomes for Indigenous students, inviting the OECD to shape and implement the study in conjunction with other interested Canadian provinces and territories.

Four provinces (Alberta, Manitoba, New Brunswick and Nova Scotia) and two territories (Northwest Territories and Yukon) took part in the study, demonstrating their strong commitment to improving educational experiences and outcomes for Indigenous students. In addition, the participating provinces and territories invited New Zealand and Queensland (Australia) to contribute to the study as a means to further enhance peer learning. Their contributions demonstrate the progress achieved in these two jurisdictions, as well as the challenges that remain.

While many representatives contributed to the study, we especially wish to thank Karen Andrews of Alberta Education, who initiated, advocated for and steered the study at every step. Her commitment to partnership and to evidence-based research to achieve sustained educational improvement for Indigenous students is unwavering. We also want to thank all the representatives who contributed to the study (see the full list in Annex B). Each ministry/department provided considerable input, completing complex and detailed questionnaires on the data they hold on well-being, participation, engagement and achievement of Indigenous students. They also provided information on the strategies, policies and programmes currently in place to improve educational experiences and outcomes for Indigenous students, as well as other relevant research and evidence.

The representatives contributed significantly to the design and development of the study. In addition to two two-day face-to-face meetings, they participated in webinars and provided detailed comments on drafts of the report. Their feedback and guidance is much appreciated. We are also indebted to the provinces and territories for hosting us and organising meetings with key stakeholders, including visits to schools and meetings with Indigenous Elders and other leaders.

Thanks are also due to Tony Dreise and Bill Perrett, of the Australian Council for Educational Research, who completed a comprehensive literature review of evidence and case studies on the well-being, participation, engagement and achievement of Indigenous children and young people in education.

We also want to express our sincere gratitude to all the Indigenous students, parents and teachers we met in the course of the study. They generously shared their knowledge and insights on the experiences of Indigenous children and their families in their provincial/territorial education systems. They talked with us about past and current wrongs in the education systems, the developments that are positive for Indigenous student and their aspirations for the future. We clearly heard frustration with the lack of progress, but we also heard hope for the future.

Andreas Schleicher

Director for Education and Skills and Special Advisor
on Education Policy to the Secretary-General
OECD

Acknowledgements

David Istance, Senior Analyst in the OECD Directorate for Education and Skills, prepared the chapters on the approach, objectives and methodology of the study, its context and student well-being. Rowena Phair, Project Leader in the OECD Directorate for Education and Skills, led the study, wrote the other chapters and finalised the report. Judith Peterka provided input in the early stages, including development of the questionnaire and research design, and carried out the field visits in Canada with David Istance and Rowena Phair. Peggy Furic completed most of the quantitative analysis, drafted some sections of the report and assisted in finalising the report. Andreas Schleicher, Paulo Santiago and Richard Yelland provided oversight, direction and valuable advice on content and process. Susan Copeland edited the text and Célia Braga-Schich handled logistics and formatting. In addition, Lindsey Ricker contributed to some aspects of the project.

Table of contents

Boxes

Tables

Executive summary

Four Canadian provinces (Alberta, Manitoba, New Brunswick and Nova Scotia) and two territories (Northwest Territories and Yukon) participated in this study, along with New Zealand and Queensland (Australia).[1] They all are actively seeking to better meet the educational needs and aspirations of Indigenous students and their families, reflecting the priority each of these jurisdictions places on improving outcomes for Indigenous peoples. This also recognises the United Nations Declaration on the Rights of Indigenous Peoples 2007, which all three countries have endorsed.

The study focuses primarily on the participating Canadian provinces and territories. New Zealand and Queensland participated as peer countries, sharing their experiences and insights. Field visits were made to each of the participating Canadian jurisdictions, but not to New Zealand or Queensland. The study also focuses only on education under the jurisdiction of the Canadian provinces and territories. It does not include education provided by the Canadian federal government or directly by First Nation communities.

The objectives of the study are threefold: 1) to identify promising strategies, policies, programmes and practices that support improved learning outcomes for Indigenous students; 2) to build an empirical evidence base on what works to better support Indigenous students to succeed in education; and 3) to assist provinces and territories in Canada to learn from one another as they strive to achieve sustained and accelerated progress in closing education gaps for Indigenous students.

The study seeks to identify promising practices and policies that are effectively supporting the well-being, participation, engagement and achievement in education of Indigenous students. These four outcomes are interconnected and mutually reinforcing. They provide the basis for the research design and the analytical lens for this study. They also provide a means for the participating education systems to measure their progress towards better student outcomes. While academic success is important, progress on student well-being, participation and engagement in learning both benefits students directly and supports improvements in student achievement.

Key findings

A clear will to improve

In the participating provinces and territories there is a clear will and strong commitment among officials and stakeholders at every level to improve education outcomes for Indigenous students. This is evidenced by the range of new initiatives and programmes being put in place across participating jurisdictions and the focus on Indigenous students within each ministry. Almost all Canadian provinces and territories are implementing changes to the school curriculum, associated resource materials and learning activities offered to students. Visible progress is also being achieved in the processes of engagement between education ministries and schools with Indigenous communities. In addition, a range of responses have been put in place to address challenges such as remoteness and poverty, which can disproportionately affect Indigenous students and hinder students' access to high-quality education.

Many promising practices are evident

In the field research for this study, the research team visited a number of Canadian schools that are achieving highly positive outcomes for Indigenous students at an individual school level, using approaches that could be replicated to some extent in other schools. There was a common formula in these schools: an inspirational leader; strong relationships with students, parents and local communities; capable and committed staff; the use of every possible lever to engage and support students to be successful; and sustained commitment to achieve improvements.

The practices that benefit Indigenous students also benefit non-Indigenous students

Schools achieving sound results for Indigenous students also tend to do so for non-Indigenous students. All students benefit from high-quality, responsive teaching in combination with localised curriculum and learning activities, within a safe and inclusive school environment. Successful schools mainstream local Indigenous values, history and cultural approaches as part of everyday school life, rather than add-ons targeted only to Indigenous students.

Achieving change at a system level requires deliberate, sustained effort

The study also identifies areas where system-level improvements have been achieved for Indigenous students. These include improvements to students' sense of well-being in education, their likelihood of participating and engaging in education, and their achievements in education. Examples of system-wide improvements span from early childhood education and care (ECEC) to senior schooling. Across the policies and practices that have had a significantly positive impact, there are some common elements in achieving this success. These include:

- setting deliberate, measurable targets and reporting on them
- taking multiple actions at both system and local levels
- persisting and adjusting efforts over a significant period of time.

An underlying ingredient for success is having access to reliable, regular and up-to-date data to monitor progress on the goals being pursued.

Priorities for accelerating change

Drawing on the promising policies and practices identified in this study, we recommend six system-level priorities to bring about positive change in the educational experiences of Indigenous students. These are set out below.

Student well-being

The well-being of all students is a critical and desirable outcome, fundamental to students' ability to participate, engage with and succeed in education. The research team is aware that individual schools in the participating jurisdictions monitor the well-being of all students (for example, the OurSCHOOL evaluation instrument in Canada and the *Rongohia te Hau* survey tool, part of *Kia Eke Panuku*[2], in New Zealand). However, only one jurisdiction monitors the well-being of Indigenous students on a jurisdiction-wide basis, over time. Given the negative experiences of many Indigenous peoples in education, it is surprising that there is no systematic monitoring of the well-being of Indigenous students in schools.

Participation rates

Both New Zealand and Queensland have achieved improvements in Indigenous students' participation in education through deliberate efforts. Such improvements have provided opportunities for Indigenous students to learn critical skills and have a chance of succeeding in education that they would not have had without such systemic intervention. The largest gains in participation rates tend to be needed in both ECEC and the senior years of education.

Student engagement

Students vote with their feet, and they also respond to expectations. If students do not attend school regularly, they reduce their opportunities to learn, fall behind and lose confidence and interest in learning. It is a negative, downward spiral. While some Canadian schools are achieving sound attendance rates among Indigenous students, other schools are struggling and are unable to achieve improvements on their own. Student attendance was raised by teachers as the issue that they feel would have the most impact on improving Indigenous students' success in education.

Both New Zealand and Queensland have shown that more positive rates of student attendance can be achieved. Such gains have been made through systemic monitoring at central and local levels and corresponding action at both levels.

Early learning

Indigenous children are less likely to participate in ECEC and to start school later than other students. This means that a potentially powerful lever to lift student achievement is not being used to full effect. Providing high-quality ECEC that is responsive to the needs of individual children and their families can significantly boost students' achievement levels in later schooling. ECEC is the single most powerful lever for achieving a step change within a generation.

Models of ECEC that respond to children's needs and are located within Indigenous communities do exist within the Canadian jurisdictions participating in this study, including ECEC services operating off-reserve. Making such provision available for as many Indigenous children as possible should be a priority for all Canadian jurisdictions in their efforts to boost the educational outcomes of these students.

Supporting teachers and leaders

Every school we visited that was achieving sound results for Indigenous students had a highly effective and committed school principal and teachers who were doing whatever it takes to support students in their learning. But they were doing it on their own. The research team did not find one Canadian school that had teamed with any other school to learn from one another or to accelerate progress.

Progress will be faster if school leaders and teachers can learn from one another and if their professional preparation and ongoing professional development effectively prepare them for all the students they work with. Some jurisdictions specify expectations for teachers and school leaders, some provide tailored professional development, and others support schools to work together to improve student outcomes. These efforts can make a difference, if they affect the practices of teaching and learning at the level of individual teachers and students.

Engaging families

Where respect, trust and positive relationships have not always been part of historic or recent experiences, families are likely to be wary of engaging with school staff. However, where bridges are built and mutually respectful relationships are formed, the benefits for students can be huge. Schools that work alongside parents as partners achieve gains in student well-being, participation, engagement and achievement.

There are a number of successful models on how schools have effectively engaged families in their children's education. The most effective are those that link schools with parents on education goals for individual students, and where parents are supported to play a very active role in their child's learning.

Conclusions

We are confident that the findings, practices, approaches and priorities identified in this study can help to achieve and accelerate progress. We would question, however, whether there is sufficient breadth and intensity system-wide to achieve the Truth and Reconciliation Commission of Canada's recommendation that the education achievement gap be closed within one generation. Achieving sustained, significant, positive change requires persistent effort on many fronts by as many people as possible.

To ensure that progress is being achieved on a system-wide basis, and that the pace of this progress is satisfactory, decision-makers and stakeholders must have access to high-quality and timely data on key indicators. While improvements in the scope and quality of data have been achieved in recent years, in most cases the data are insufficient to monitor progress with confidence over time.

Notes

1. See Annex A for an overview of the education systems in Canada, Australia and New Zealand.

2. The name *Kia Eke Panuku* uses a metaphor that encapsulates a journey towards success that is both dynamic and continuous, building from a school's current situation to where it aspires to be for Māori students and their home communities. For further information, see *"Kia Eke Panuku: Building on Success 2013-2016"*, http://kep.org.nz/assets/resources/site/Voices7-1.Rongohia-te-Hau.pdf.

Chapter 1

Overview: Improving the educational experiences of Indigenous students

This chapter presents an overview of the factors and priorities identified in this study as critical to improving the educational experiences of Indigenous students. A number of factors support and enable significant, sustained improvement at system, community and school levels. These include respecting the rights and values of Indigenous students, setting targets with firm time frames, working closely with individual students and their families and communities, and collecting data to monitor progress over time. At the system level, three initiatives in particular should be included in any strategy to improve the education experiences of Indigenous students: providing high-quality early learning opportunities; supporting teachers and leaders to develop awareness, capability and confidence; and monitoring progress across key indicators at both system and school levels. At the individual school level, the combination of priorities used will differ depending on circumstances, but at a minimum, schools should focus on: quality and effectiveness of teaching; engagement with families; and direct support for students. The issues faced by Indigenous students go far beyond education, but it is education that provides hope and promise to address disparities, not only in educational opportunities but also a much wider set of inequities.

"It's our responsibility to find the resources we need … these are children, who want to learn." **(School principal, New Brunswick)**

Indigenous peoples are diverse, within and across nations. The Indigenous peoples in the three countries in this study, however, have experienced colonisation processes that undermined Indigenous young people's access to their identity, language and culture. At the same time, Indigenous children have not generally had access to the same quality of education that other children in their country enjoy. These two forces in combination have undermined the educational opportunities and outcomes of successive generations of Indigenous children and young people, at times with catastrophic effect.

The legacy of colonisation processes, including residential schools, means that improving the educational experiences and outcomes of Indigenous students is challenging and complex. The issues faced by Indigenous students go far beyond education, but it is education that provides hope and promise to address disparities, not only in educational opportunities but also a much wider set of inequities.

In a similar vein, education systems that have not been designed to recognise and respond to the needs and contexts of Indigenous students will take time to adjust. School leaders and teachers have not always been effectively prepared to teach Indigenous students, nor are they necessarily provided with the resources to help them develop their capabilities and their confidence.

There are no quick fixes in improving education outcomes for any group of students, and this is also true for Indigenous students. Evidence from improvements and successes that have been achieved for Indigenous students clearly point to strategies that are deliberate in intent, open and flexible in approach, vigilant in monitoring progress, and sustained in effort over time.

To achieve significant and sustained improvement

In investigating system-level improvements and those at a community or school level, we have identified a number of factors that support and enable significant, sustained improvement, as set out below.

Relationships and respect

A foundation for effecting positive change is to recognise and respect the rights, agency and value of Indigenous students, their families and their communities. Building effective relationships relies on mutual trust and respect. Schools that have achieved sustained improvements for Indigenous students recognise the key role of Indigenous parents, leaders and other community members and have actively built relationships with these important people in their students' lives. In some cases, formal agreements are reached between education leaders and Indigenous leaders, such as Education Enhancement Agreements in some Canadian provinces and territories. These set out common objectives and commitments, in terms of the expected provision of education for Indigenous students.

Deliberate intent

A common way to motivate and instigate action is to set targets for the level of improvements to be achieved within a given timeframe. Targets alone are not sufficient to achieve progress, but they have helped jurisdictions to address the question of "what it will take" to achieve the objectives they set and to monitor progress over time. Without such targets, it is easier to focus only on the actions being taken, rather than the on impact of those actions.

Action on several fronts

It is not easy to address deep, intergenerational and systemic issues. Implementing only one or two initiatives or policy changes is unlikely to bring about significant improvements at a system level. In schools that have achieved significant improvements, a number of strategies and actions have been implemented, rather than any single response. This is also the case for achievement of system-level improvements, such as on participation and qualifications outcomes. Thus, it is a combination of actions that enables Indigenous students to be sufficiently supported to benefit from high-quality education, rather than only one or two policies or programmes.

At system and local levels

System-level actions are necessary, but they are seldom sufficient to change the educational experiences and outcomes of individual students. System-level efforts can initiate and enable change at the local level, but it is the quality, breadth and depth of the local provision that determine whether there is an impact on students. However, much can be done at the system level to support and incentivise school leaders and teachers to improve their approaches.

Working with individual students

To change the experiences of individual students, it is generally necessary to work directly with each student and his/her family or community. Individual needs are diverse and change over time, so it is often necessary to carry out continuous tracking at the school level, especially for students at risk of disengaging. In this way, schools and education advisors develop a better understanding of the barriers and risks that students face, barriers that may not be apparent without such individualised data.

Sufficient effort to make a difference

The effort needs to be commensurate with the improvement goal and the size of the target population. For example, an Indigenous Worker based in one school, with a mandate to work with its students and their families and teachers, can have a significant positive impact, while spreading the same resource over a number of schools will not have the same impact.

Over a sustained period

The schools and jurisdictions in this study that have achieved sustained improvements have all pursued consistent objectives for at least a ten year period. The strategies followed to achieve the objectives have sometimes been refined or changed over this period, but the basic objectives have been retained. However, three to five years is a reasonable time frame in which improvements should be visible. If improvements are not seen in this period, it is likely that the strategies used are not sufficiently targeted to changes in practice, are not comprehensive or are not adequately resourced to make a difference to students' actual experiences.

Data to monitor progress

Monitoring progress helps to see whether the package of initiatives in place has sufficient breadth and reach to affect student outcomes. This will demonstrate the value of the current strategies and also motivate any additional efforts that may be needed. Without data to monitor progress, it is easy to become convinced that progress is being achieved, especially if the new initiatives have wide support. The data also help to build capability at both system and school levels, in the expectations for success and the skills required to affect change. Such information can also build demand among parents and students, in terms of their expectations, voice and influence.

System-level priorities

Effort is needed at both system and school levels. In some areas, however, action can only be taken – or is best taken – at the system level. This can be because responsibilities match the role and mandate of the central agency rather than schools, or because it is more efficient to carry out actions centrally rather than locally. Drawing on the experiences and evidence of where improvements have been achieved in these Canadian provinces and territories and in New Zealand and Queensland, the study has identified a number of system-level priorities that have supported progress for Indigenous students. Figure 1.1 groups these according to the likely impact on student outcomes and likely cost[1].

Figure 1.1. System-level priorities supporting progress for Indigenous students, likely impact on student outcomes and cost

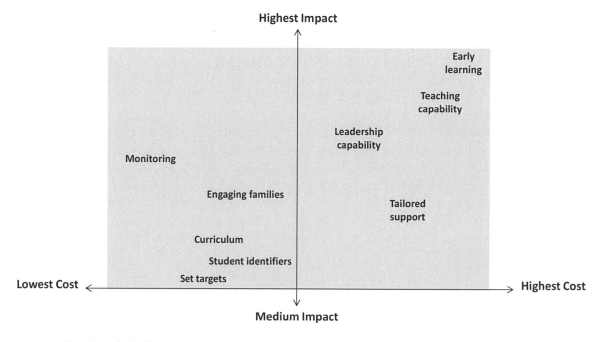

Each jurisdiction in this study is unique in terms of current pressures, initiatives already in place or in development, and the priorities of their Indigenous and education communities. Thus, the combination of priorities, policies and initiatives that each jurisdiction pursues must be a matter for each to determine in its own way.

There are, however, three system-level initiatives in particular, discussed below, that we believe should be included in any strategy to improve the education experiences of Indigenous students:

- providing high-quality early learning opportunities
- supporting teachers and leaders to develop awareness, capability and confidence
- monitoring progress at system and school levels across key indicators.

Early learning

Indigenous children are more likely to not participate in ECEC and have a later start in school than other students. This means a potentially powerful lever to lift student achievement is not being used to full effect. The provision of high quality early childhood education and care (ECEC) that is responsive to the needs of individual children and their families, can significantly lift students' achievement levels in later schooling. This is the single most powerful lever for achieving a step change within a generation.

Models of ECEC that respond to children's needs and that are located within Indigenous communities do exist within the Canadian jurisdictions that participated in this study. Making such provision available for as many Indigenous children as possible should be a priority for all jurisdictions in their efforts to boost the educational outcomes of these students.

An example of such an approach is a centre in North Winnipeg (Manitoba) that is targeted to children with multiple risk factors. The centre is located at the heart of an impoverished, predominantly Indigenous community. The centre follows an Abecedarian model of early development and learning, which is an intense, individualised, relations-based approach. Families are an integral part of the programme, which includes home visits by centre staff and encouraging parents' involvement in the centre. The centre also actively recruits and trains local staff, resulting in lower turnover than would otherwise be the case and greater trust between parents and staff.

Supporting teachers and leaders

Every school we visited for this study that was achieving sound results for Indigenous students had a highly effective and committed school principal and teachers who were doing whatever it takes to support students in their learning, but they were doing it on their own. The research team did not meet one school that had teamed with any other school to learn from one another or to accelerate progress.

Progress will be faster if school leaders and teachers can learn from one another, and if their professional preparation and ongoing professional development effectively prepare them for all the students they are required to work with. Some jurisdictions specify expectations for teachers and school leaders, some provide tailored professional development, and others support schools to work together to improve student outcomes. These efforts can make a difference, if they affect the practices of teaching and learning at the level of individual teachers and students.

An example from New Zealand where progress has been achieved, including for Indigenous students, is through the Learning and Change Networks. Schools voluntarily work together to boost student achievement in particular learning areas. The programme involves teachers from different schools interrogating data from their own and other schools, classroom observations across schools, involvement of students' views on their learning, and persistence in achieving mutual goals over a number of years. This collaborative approach has led to a New Zealand-wide initiative, Communities of

Learning, to incentivise and assist more schools to work together for the benefit of their students. Communities of learning aim to enhance the quality of teaching, education career pathways for teachers and education leaderships.

Monitoring progress

It is essential to monitor progress to be able to make adjustments to the suite of policies and other initiatives being implemented. Data on overall outcomes such as participation and completion rates can only be produced at a system level, rather than at the level of individual schools. Thus, an overview of the nature and rate of progress is only possible if central education agencies take responsibility for this.

Data collection and monitoring can also be combined effectively with education targets, creating an accountability mechanism for the performance of the system as a whole in relation to Indigenous students. Indigenous Elders we spoke to in the course of this study proposed such an accountability system as a way of establishing system-level responsibility for Indigenous student outcomes. An example of such a mechanism is the annual "Closing the Gap report" produced by the Australian Department of Prime Minister and Cabinet.

School-level priorities

The line of sight to each student is much clearer at the local level than from a system-level perspective, as are the quality and effectiveness of the teaching strategies applied in each classroom. In addition, schools are able to engage with Indigenous families and communities in a more relational and ongoing way than system-level initiatives can do. Using the lens of likely impact and cost, Figure 1.2 below summarises the priorities we would expect schools to consider to boost education outcomes for Indigenous students.

Figure 1.2. School-level priorities to boost education outcomes for Indigenous students, likely impact and cost

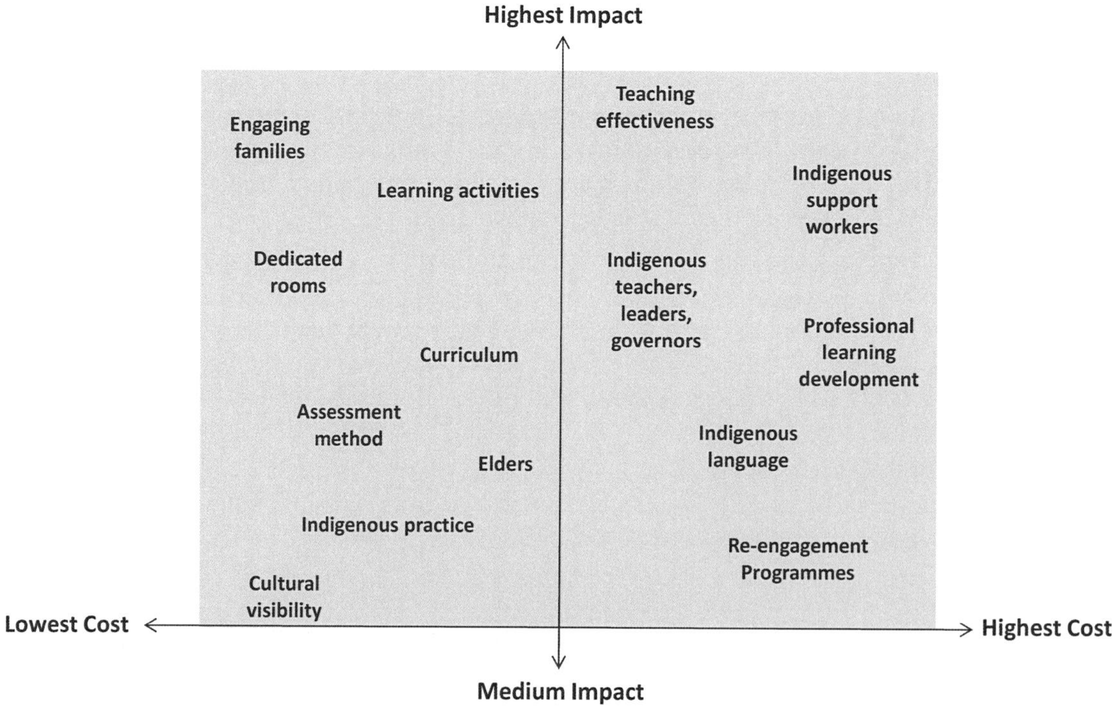

Again, just as the circumstances of each school will differ, the combination of priorities used at an individual school level will and should differ. At a minimum, however, we believe schools should focus on:

- quality and effectiveness of teaching

- engagement with families

- direct support for students.

Quality and effectiveness of teaching

There are many aspects to high-quality and effective teaching in different settings. In the context of Indigenous students, we found that teachers' expectations of students' capability and success are critical to whether students progress well or not. Teachers are sometimes unaware of the assumptions they are making about their students, especially if there are cultural or linguistic differences between themselves and their students. However, such assumptions can change when teachers become aware of their preconceptions, including the impact these have on their students.

Teaching can be enhanced through the deliberate selection of learning activities, curriculum content and assessment mechanisms. These can be used in many ways to make learning more relevant and engaging for Indigenous students and to build their confidence and competence.

Engaging families

Where respect, trust and positive relationships have not always been part of historic or recent experiences, families are likely to be wary of engaging with school staff. However, where bridges are built and mutually respectful relationships are formed, the benefits for students can be significant. Schools that work alongside parents as partners achieve gains in student well-being, participation, engagement and achievement.

There are a number of successful models of how schools have effectively engaged families in their children's education. The most effective are those that link schools with parents on education goals for individual students and where parents are supported to play a very active role in their child's learning.

Direct support for students

There are many ways to provide direct support to individual students. A model that works well for schools with a number of Indigenous students is Indigenous Support Workers. Such staff can effectively address barriers faced by Indigenous students and identify opportunities to increase their engagement and success in education. More specifically, such staff can contribute to ensuring the regular participation of Indigenous students, supporting teachers in building sound relationships with Indigenous students and their parents, initiating new curriculum resources, and leading professional development for teachers and whole-of-school activities.

Schools with few Indigenous students or without the resources to hire an Indigenous Support Worker can obtain some benefits from sharing an Indigenous Support Worker with other schools or use other means, such as engaging the support and advice from Indigenous Elders and other community leaders, and through distributing responsibilities across existing staff.

Note

1. Note that the relative impacts and cost of each priority and their position in the Figure 1.1 draw on findings in this study, other OECD research and an assessment of this range of information by the authors of this report.

Chapter 2

Approach, objectives and methodology of the study on Indigenous students and education

This study aims to understand the experiences of Indigenous students and to identify successful strategies, policies and practices to support their success. Four Canadian provinces and two territories participated in the study, and New Zealand and Queensland (Australia) provided data and other information to enrich the study. The report looks beyond student attainment and achievement to include well-being, participation and engagement. Well-being is a very prominent consideration from an Indigenous perspective, and it is of key importance to any approach to student success. Indigenous perspectives need to be genuinely recognised and not be considered as simply an add-on to the main goals of education. In fact, those perspectives fit closely with aims informing educational development around the world, including the major global objectives for education, of the UN Sustainable Development Goals. While we have sought policies and practices underpinned by evidence of success, the lack of evaluation is problematic regarding education for Indigenous populations.

This history of Indigenous people's experiences is not universally understood, as the 2015 Truth and Reconciliation Commission of Canada has so powerfully stated. The Commission was established with the mandate to inform all Canadians about what happened in Indian residential schools, as part of a process of reconciliation and renewed relationships based on mutual understanding and respect.[1] In its review of the negative impacts of Canada's residential schools, the Commission recommended that the education achievement gap between Indigenous and non-Indigenous students be closed in one generation. This recommendation has provided further impetus to provinces and territories to work together to make faster and more certain progress. Education provides hope and builds agency and voice. It supports students to lead the lives they wish and to pursue and achieve their chosen goals, for themselves, their families and their communities.

Indigenous peoples represented 4.3% of the total Canadian population in 2011 (Statistics Canada, 2016), 3% of the total Australian population in 2014 (Australian Bureau of Statistics, 2015) and 15.6% of the total New Zealand population in 2013 (Statistics New Zealand, 2015). The Indigenous populations in the three countries are each growing at a faster rate and have a younger age structure than non-Indigenous populations. In Canada, for example, the number of people self-identifying as Indigenous increased by approximately 20% between 2006 and 2011, compared to 5% for those self-identifying as non-Indigenous (Statistics Canada, 2015). Thus, in addition to other compelling reasons to improve Indigenous students' outcomes, if educational outcomes for Indigenous students do not improve and the proportion of Indigenous students continues to increase, the overall education performance of each country will decline. And this will have negative flow-on effects to both social and economic outcomes at a societal level.

Objectives

This study aims to understand and frame the experiences of Indigenous students and to identify successful strategies, policies and practices to support improvements and their success. Four Canadian provinces (Alberta, Manitoba, New Brunswick and Nova Scotia) and two territories (Northwest Territories and Yukon) took part in the study, demonstrating their strong commitment to improving educational experiences and outcomes for Indigenous students.

In addition, the participating provinces and territories invited New Zealand and Queensland (Australia) to contribute to the study as a means to further enhance peer learning. They each have significant Indigenous communities, and both systems have their own histories and strategies addressing the life situations and educational outcomes of Indigenous students. The aim is not to compare directly, but to compile relevant information and inspiring examples to shed further light on the situation of Indigenous students.

The study takes a three-tiered approach. First, acknowledging the heterogeneity of Indigenous students, the study seeks to understand the complex challenges Indigenous students face in education and what success really means for them. It examines well-being, health and poverty; the presence or absence of quality approaches to teaching and student engagement; differences in basic provision that inordinately affect Indigenous students; recognition of Indigenous cultures; and engagement with Indigenous communities. The study's outcomes are related to all of these, as well as to student learning and achievement.

Second, the study examines and discusses promising policies, strategies and practices submitted to OECD by the participating jurisdictions and identifies positive conditions and drivers for success. The data and strategies cited for Canada refer only to education systems funded by provinces and territories; they do not include data and policies for First Nation schools located on-reserve.

Third, the study highlights strategies, policies and practices for which there is positive evidence of effectiveness in achieving improvements and enhancing success (although policies and practices in relation to Indigenous education are not widely evaluated, an issue discussed later in this chapter). These strategies, policies and practices, where positive impacts are evident, are termed "promising practices" in this report. The overall aim of the study is to identify approaches that might be transferable, sustainable and scalable.

Given the diverse sources and methodologies involved, and the very different states of data availability in the participating Canadian jurisdictions, this does not lead to comparative analysis placing each jurisdiction side by side on common indicators. It aims instead to show broad trends and approaches and gather insights on the different strategies, policies and practices being implemented.

Our approach is holistic. Patterns of educational success are not to be understood as simply the outcomes of narrow school variables. They also bring in a rich set of social, cultural and educational factors. What happens in one aspect of students' lives influences the other aspects.

We have sought to capture this breadth and the multifaceted nature of the issues in the analytical framework. It is important to note that the framework is circular, with achievement influenced by well-being, participation and engagement and, in turn, influencing them. At the same time, we see a natural progression, considering student well-being through educational participation, through engagement in learning, and through enhanced achievement. Each component frames the conditions and opportunities for the component that follows, providing the structure and the sequence of the report, with chapters on well-being, participation, engagement and achievement (Figure 2.1).

Figure 2.1. Analytical framework

Methodology

Analytical components of the study included: 1) an analysis of data from each participating jurisdiction on the well-being, participation, engagement and achievement of Indigenous students; 2) a synthesis of the strategies, policies and programmes being used that may benefit Indigenous students and evidence relating to these efforts; and 3) a literature review of evidence on improving education for Indigenous students, supplemented by evaluations and other research provided by participating jurisdictions.

The study used a mix of methodologies to clarify key developments and issues and structure the report:

- Compilation of materials and data original to the study from each of the participating jurisdictions and comparator systems, through specifically-designed questionnaires in three areas: 1) data on participation and enrolment, engagement, and achievement; 2) policy on pertinent strategies, initiatives and policies; and 3) relevant research undertaken in those systems and jurisdictions.

- Discussions at meetings between the lead Canadian jurisdiction (Alberta) and the OECD team, between Alberta and the other participating provinces and territories, and between those responsible for the study from these different groups. Two face-to-face meetings were held:

  - Edmonton, Alberta (2-3 February 2016) to clarify the aspirations, objectives, context and concerns of each province and territory, to shape the design of the study and to clarify the approach of the OECD.

  - Winnipeg, Manitoba (2-4 November 2016) with the participating jurisdictions (including a representative from New Zealand), primarily to give feedback on an initial draft of the report and to discuss finalisation of the report and options regarding further work in this area.

- Discussions with a selection of key stakeholders and on-site visits in each participating Canadian province and territory (May and June 2016). For each field visit, the OECD research team visited schools and met with Indigenous students and their parents, Indigenous teachers and support workers, Elders, school leaders and teachers, and other education stakeholders. The team met with more than 220 people in the course of the field visits, of whom 30%-40% are Indigenous (the team did not ask interviewees to self-identify as Indigenous or not).

- Additional commissioned research (Dreise and Perrett, forthcoming), in addition to literature identified through conventional research scanning and relevant OECD data, analysis and research.

- Synthesis of the material and analysis, the draft report, and recommendations.

The study involved the original collection of material from each participating jurisdiction, as well as a specially-commissioned research review by the Indigenous Research Unit of the Australian Council for Education Research. Through the discussions, iterations and protocols, we were able to develop confidence in the data sets. The study, designed and undertaken within a single calendar year, is intended as a relatively rapid exercise to capture the contemporary situation and developments, as is typical in OECD reviews. OECD procedures also call for on-site visits and discussions with a range of stakeholders, which of necessity are highly selective. Finally, by incorporating experience from two additional systems as well as more general literature and OECD analysis, the study is informed by international experience and perspectives.

The concurrent, mixed-method strategy enabled the collection and synthesis of qualitative and quantitative data to deepen the analysis, using multiple sources. A literature review, data questionnaires, field visits, interviews, group discussions and dialogues among representatives from all stakeholders have all been drawn on for data collection and analysis. We first explored the quantitative data and then sought to explore the qualitative field data through replication, identifying programmes that were thought to be successful and seeking replication of those characteristics of success elsewhere (Lloyd-Jones, 2003).

The questionnaires

We developed specific frameworks and associated questions for each of the three questionnaires, including questions about definitions and data availability. For the policy questionnaire, jurisdictions were invited to introduce their detailed responses with an overview, so as not to lose main strategic lines in the detail of specific initiatives. A further occasion to elaborate on the replies to the questionnaires came with the face-to-face meetings in each of the participating Canadian provinces and territories in May and June 2016.

Compilation and analysis of existing jurisdictional data

A basic part of the field work involved gathering data on and related to Indigenous students in all jurisdictions and comparator systems. Specifically, the purpose of the data questionnaire was to gather information to identify: 1) what data are available relating to Indigenous students; 2) progress and success of Indigenous students; and 3) whether the data are comparable across jurisdictions. The questionnaire covers information on participation and enrolment; engagement (attendance, expulsion, early school leaving, well-being); and achievement (jurisdiction test results, completion). As well as comparing Indigenous students with non-Indigenous students, it offers insights on differences in gender, socio-economic status and school characteristics, (including school type and geographic location), as well as students identified as having special learning needs and the learning settings for them. The questionnaires only cover existing data. Jurisdictions were not asked to gather new data or to extrapolate from data that were not immediately available.

Relevant research and evaluation

The purpose of the research questionnaire was to identify existing evidence related to Indigenous student outcomes, including significant research undertaken in participating jurisdictions or at a national level, as well as policy or programme evaluations. The questionnaire focuses on Indigenous students' educational experiences in a broad sense, at different levels. It covers large-scale or small-scale research conducted within the past 20 years, as well as research (ongoing or about to start) designed to evaluate policies or resourcing and aimed at improving the learning outcomes of Indigenous students, or to shed light on their experiences or perspectives.

Compilations of current policies and approaches

The third questionnaire aimed to identify the policies and initiatives that shape the educational experiences of Indigenous students in each jurisdiction, and influence their learning outcomes, directly or indirectly. It includes any evaluations of these policies and initiatives (although some of these may have been captured in the research questionnaire). It is divided into an overview and a request for more detailed information on the same policies and initiatives. These policies and initiatives may be in the form of laws and statutes, rules and regulations, ordinances and orders, or in the form of strategies, programmes, projects and initiatives. They may be organised by government or by stakeholders at the classroom, educational institution, school board/district, jurisdiction or national level. Those implemented since 2000 are all viewed as relevant, not just those that are very recent.

The questionnaire focuses on the following areas: 1) lifting Indigenous student achievement; 2) data and monitoring at different system levels; 3) leadership; 4) quality standards, support and development; 5) teacher policies; 6) curriculum frameworks and materials; 7) parent and family support; and 8) community engagement. It was specified that our interest was not only in programmes and initiatives specifically targeted at Indigenous students, but also those that affect all students and also have significance for the outcomes and experiences of Indigenous populations.

Defining success, closing gaps

Educational systems frequently define success in relation to education and Indigenous students and communities in terms of closing gaps, using various educational performance indicators (such as attendance, retention, transitions and academic assessments, often in literacy and numeracy or success on examinations). These are all important diagnostic measures to keep track of the progress of Indigenous students. However, the literature and debate (especially from Indigenous scholars and representative organisations) highlight distinct and broader criteria of educational and learning success, such as positive self-concept, strong cultural identity, happiness and confidence.

Indigenous communal values in family (clan/nation/tribe), history, nature, country and environment are often highlighted, both as central tenets of Indigenous communities and in contrast to the more individualistic, meritocratic mainstream values of many education systems. There is a widespread concern among Indigenous scholars and community advocates about loss of language, the importance of language and cultural preservation and revitalisation, and a desire to see greater social harmony, anti-racist sentiment and cultural respect (Dreise and Perrett, forthcoming; CCL, 2007). Indigenous research also points to identity, wisdom and traditions as critical in shaping identity and character, and sustaining deep relationships between kin, land and water.

In the face of such contrasts, it might be supposed, that a clear choice needs to be made between them – to endorse a focus either on attainment gaps or on broader and more humanistic, holistic concerns. This is not a view we share. It is necessary to focus strongly on measurable gaps, disparities and progress, using mainstream attainment and assessment measures, and also to widen perspectives to reflect Indigenous cultures and community priorities. It is also important that young people from Indigenous communities be able to walk in both worlds and be global citizens, as well as to be enriched through full recognition of and access to their own cultures, perspectives and traditions.

Avoiding deficit thinking

A point that is repeatedly stressed in the literature is the need to avoid deficit thinking, which infers that Indigenous cultures and students are lacking and assume that the task is to rectify their shortcomings and failings. However, focusing on important disparities and shortcomings when they occur should not be mistaken for deficit thinking (the superficial idea of avoiding negatives while concentrating exclusively on good news). This point was underlined in the OECD report *Doing Better for Children* (OECD, 2009), concluding that it is very important to address inequalities while also focusing on strengths:

> [The] ... divide in the child well-being literature is between those who place a focus on poor child well-being outcomes and those who prefer to conceive of child well-being as a positive continuous variable. The latter group sometimes describe the former approach as a "deficit approach" and their own approach as a "strengths-based" one (Ben-Arieh and Goerge, 2001; Pollard and Lee, 2003; Fattore, Mason and Watson, 2007) ... A focus on deficits is often criticised in the academic literature. Taking a "deficit approach" is used pejoratively. However, there are some very good reasons why policy makers may choose to focus on well-being for children in terms of so-called deficit measures. These policy reasons encompass both efficiency and equity rationales.
>
> [...]
>
> However, it certainly remains the case that relying only on deficit measures misses the positive strengths and abilities that children possess, and on which society must build to enhance child well-being. (OECD, 2009, pp.25-26)

This report sees it as crucial to include a focus on disparities and progress in order to overcome them, although we would not call that deficit thinking. The important point is to avoid analyses that assume that the challenges reside primarily or exclusively with the Indigenous populations themselves, do not have implications for the non-Indigenous populations and do not recognise the diverse rights, strengths and positives of the Indigenous communities. The point of departure cannot be that of blaming students and their families, as opposed to systems and structures. Similar problems arise with the term "closing gaps" in that it risks not questioning the dimensions on which gaps are being measured, and ignoring that many non-Indigenous students are also struggling in relation to the same indicators.

In addressing the meaning of success, we would emphasise that it is not about privileging one world view at the expense of another, but rather of properly recognising Indigenous cultures, values and perspectives while laying the foundations for young Indigenous students to be able to participate actively in the wider society and economy and the global world (to walk in both worlds). We have stressed the need to address the harsh and often stubborn gaps in such dimensions as participation, engagement and achievement, while at the same time problematising these gaps and focusing on positive measures that build on strengths. Inequalities reflect deep-seated social and historical patterns, rather than being understood as characteristics that attach to individuals and groups as flaws to be compensated for. We recognise the extent to which problems can be related to poverty or providing quality education in remote areas rather than assuming that they are specific to Indigenous populations *per se.*

Indigenous approaches integral to global reform and innovation

We can go further than this. Far from being marginal to mainstream concerns, Indigenous values and approaches are increasingly being pursued as global directions for educational policies in the 21st century, although such alignment is rarely recognised in mainstream debate. If it were, approaches would automatically shift from deficit thinking towards strengths. In fact, approaches and perspectives associated with Indigenous communities are in the process of being integrated into global contemporary discourse as defining the way ahead.

A good example is the pursuit of lifelong learning. This is integral to Indigenous cultures, including through non-formal learning. Governments around the world have long espoused the principles of lifelong learning, even while struggling with major policy challenges in converting the rhetoric into reality. The seminal 1996 UNESCO Commission report on lifelong learning (the Delors Report) still stands as one of the most ambitious and impressive statements (UNESCO, 1996). It maintained the primacy of four fundamental pillars of learning: 1) learning to know; 2) learning to do; 3) learning to be; and 4) learning to live together. This holistic agenda, which is so consistent with the philosophies of Indigenous populations, was thus recognised two decades ago as setting the terms for learning in the 21st century. Lifelong learning enjoys a prominent place in the 2015 UN Sustainable Development Goal on education.

Sliwka and Yee (2015) recently analysed the extent to which innovative education, including alternative education, is already reshaping mainstream policy, examining alternatives that place high priorities on recognition of place, relevance, emotions and engagement. They suggest that principles that align with those of Indigenous peoples have been increasingly adopted in mainstream reforms, in Germany and Canada and beyond. They see this as entirely consistent with what is known from research about what makes for powerful learning:

> In line with research on human development, schools in public school systems across the OECD are increasingly broadening their philosophy of teaching to create settings for learning, which aim at the integration of cognitive, metacognitive and social-emotional development of learners at the same time. (p.175)

Their thinking finds a strong echo within the educational concerns of the OECD. The learning principles identified in the influential volume, *The Nature of Learning: Using Research to Inspire Practice* (Dumont, Istance and Benevides, 2010), include the important role of emotions, the social nature of learning, and the horizontal connections between the learning that goes on in school and that which takes place out of school. The importance of social and emotional learning is increasingly recognised and features strongly in OECD reflections on Education 2030. The OECD Programme for International Student Assessment (PISA), is increasingly extending towards global competence, moving away from being narrowly cognitive or focused on basics:

> Global competence is the capacity to analyse global and intercultural issues critically and from multiple perspectives, to understand how differences affect perceptions, judgments, and ideas of self and others, and to engage in open, appropriate and effective interactions with others from different backgrounds on the basis of a shared respect for human dignity. (OECD, 2016, p.4)

In short, there is increasing recognition of the need for everyone to move beyond the simpler summaries and proxies of attainment and achievement to those in which the relational dimension and respect for dignity are critical.

In looking towards the future, the major recent global event, in education, as in other fields, has been the adoption of the UN Sustainable Development Goals (SDGs). These define key global targets to be achieved by 2030, replacing the Millennium Development Goals that ran to 2015. The SDGs, adopted in September 2015, aim to end poverty, protect the planet and ensure prosperity for all, as part of a new sustainable development agenda. Each goal has specific targets to be achieved over the next 15 years.

SDG Goal 4 is on education: "Ensure inclusive and equitable quality education and promote lifelong learning opportunities for all". Target 4.5 explicitly refers to Indigenous peoples and the need to close gaps and eliminate disparities. But it also and critically includes Target 4.7, which is about creating the glue that binds all 17 of the large goals together – sustainable development – and the role that education can and should play to achieve this:

> By 2030, ensure that all learners acquire the knowledge and skills needed to promote sustainable development, including, among others, through education for sustainable development and sustainable lifestyles, human rights, gender equality, promotion of a culture of peace and non-violence, global citizenship, and appreciation of cultural diversity and of culture's contribution to sustainable development. (United Nations, 2015)

This again emphasises that the focus on sustainability which so imbues the culture and thinking of Indigenous peoples has become mainstream and indeed an urgent and prominent objective. All governments around the world have endorsed it, and they have also recognised the critical role of education to achieve it.

The weak evaluation evidence base

Evaluations in Indigenous education are especially problematic, as recognised by researchers and advocates in Indigenous education around the globe. Raham (2009) in Canada, for instance, notes that Indigenous educational research tends to be scattered, uneven in rigour, largely qualitative and often small in scale. Raham also suggests that the wider applicability of the available research is often limited due to the highly diverse range of contexts in which educational services are delivered. The lack of evaluative evidence is widely seen as a fundamental weakness when seeking to redress the manifold inequities. As summarised by Dreise and Perrett (forthcoming):

> Purdie and Buckley (2010) in Australia have also outlined an extensive case for improving the nature of the data collected in Indigenous education, including through rigorous and independent evaluations of education programmes. They cite a number of Indigenous education initiatives in Australia that have not been subjected to independent, publicly available or longitudinal evaluations. Further, they propose a key question for researchers and policy makers to address: "What constitutes reliable evidence to evaluate programmes and initiatives so that good policy and actions can be formulated to effect change?" Similarly, Friesen and Krauth (2012) in Canada have reached a general conclusion that limited evidence (especially in the form of quantitative evaluation) is holding back improvements in Indigenous education (p.6).

We confronted the lack of evaluative evidence in our study, as the evaluation questions in our questionnaires were largely left unanswered. It has constrained our ability to attain the third aim of the study, to highlight strategies, policies and practices for which there is evidence of making improvements and enhancing success.

We would not, however, underestimate the challenges confronting such evaluations, quite apart from the expertise and resources needed to undertake them. Each of the areas covered by this report is complex. The goals for learning extend well beyond simply raising achievement levels, and this is especially important as regards Indigenous education, as discussed above. The embracing concept of well-being is multidimensional and complex. Collecting data or undertaking research must be done in partnerships to avoid being viewed negatively by Indigenous groups/organisations, as such data have so often been used against their interests. Moreover, jurisdictions are implementing diverse approaches, targeted directly to Indigenous students or to all students, and that limits the transferability of conclusions regarding the impact of specific initiatives or policies. In these circumstances, the sheer number of relevant dimensions and criteria that might be used and the diversity of measures taken sets an imposing challenge for evaluation, as does the challenge of measuring those that are retained.

In working towards frameworks on how evaluation might be carried out, and in line with the strong emphasis placed on dialogue in Indigenous education, we can draw on clarification work on evaluation and innovation completed for the OECD (Earl and Timperley, 2015). They see educational evaluation as involving the systematic collection and analysis of the information needed to make decisions and identify the effects of educational initiatives and call this "evaluative thinking". This is essential to successful innovation as a disciplined process of problem definition, horizon scanning, situation analysis, monitoring of progress, creation of contingency plans and feedback for improvement throughout the innovation process. They see it as a constant process rather than a one-off, and one that actively involves the different stakeholders.

Note

1. For further information on the Truth and Reconciliation Commission of Canada, see: www.trc.ca.

References

Australian Bureau of Statistics (2015), "Estimates of Aboriginal and Torres Strait Islander Australians", www.abs.gov.au/ausstats/abs@.nsf/mf/3238.0.55.001.

Ben-Arieh, A. and R. Goerge, (2001), "Beyond the Numbers: How do We Monitor the State of Our Children?", *Children and Youth Services Review*, Vol. 23, No. 8, pp. 603-631, www.researchgate.net/publication/4822762_Beyond_the_numbers_How _do_we_monitor_the_state_of_our_children_Children_and_Youth_Services_ Review_238_603-631.

CCL (Canadian Council on Learning) (2007), "Redefining How Success is Measured in First Nations, Inuit and Métis Learning", Report on Learning in Canada 2007, CCL, Ottawa, www.afn.ca/uploads/files/education/5._2007_redefining_how_success_is_ measured_en.pdf.

Dreise, T. and W. Perrett (forthcoming), "Promising Practices in Closing the Gap in Indigenous Education: A Literature Review Report for the OECD", OECD Publishing, Paris.

Dumont, H., D. Istance and F. Benavides (eds.) (2010), *The Nature of Learning: Using Research to Inspire Practice*, OECD Publishing, Paris, http://dx.doi.org/10.1787/ 9789264086487-en.

Earl, L. and H. Timperley (2015), "Evaluative thinking for successful educational innovation", *OECD Education Working Papers*, No.122, OECD Publishing, Paris, http://dx.doi.org/ 10.1787/5jrxtk1jtdwf-en.

Fattore, T., J. Mason and E. Watson (2007), "Children's Conceptualisation(s) of their Well-being", *Social Indicators Research*, Vol. 80, pp. 105-132.

Friesen, J. and B. Krauth (2012), *Key Policy Issues in Aboriginal Education: An Evidence-Based Approach*, Council of Ministers of Education, Canada, Toronto, www.cmec.ca/Publications/Lists/Publications/Attachments/295/Key-Policy-Issues-in-Aboriginal-Education_EN.pdf.

Lloyd-Jones, G. (2003), "Design and Control Issues in Qualitative Case Study Research", *International Journal of Qualitative Methods* 2 (2), Article 4, www.ualberta.ca/~iiqm/ backissues/2_2/pdf/lloydjones.pdf.

OECD (2016), "Global Competency for an Inclusive World" (brochure), OECD, Paris, www.oecd.org/education/Global-competency-for-an-inclusive-world.pdf.

OECD (2009), *Doing Better for Children*, OECD Publishing, Paris, http://dx.doi.org/10.1787/9789264059344-en.

Pollard, E.L. and P.D. Lee (2003), "Child Well-being: A Systematic Review of the Literature", *Social Indicators Research*, Vol. 61, pp. 59-78.

Purdie, N. and S. Buckley (2010), *School attendance and retention of Indigenous Australian students,* Issues Paper No. 1 produced for the Closing the Gap Clearinghouse, Australian Government, Australian Institute of Health and Welfare and Australian Institute of Family Studies, www.aihw.gov.au/uploadedFiles/Closing TheGap/Content/Publications/2010/ctg-ip01.pdf.

Raham, H. (2009), *Best Practices in Aboriginal Education: A Literature Review and Analysis for Policy Directions*, On behalf of the Office of the Federal Interlocutor, Indian and Northern Affairs Canada, www.firstpeoplesgroup.com/mnsiurban/PDF/ education/Best_Practices_in_Aboriginal_Education-2009.pdf.

Sliwka, A. and B. Yee (2015*)*, "From Alternative Education to The Mainstream: Approaches in Canada and Germany to Preparing Learners to live in a Changing World", *European Journal of Education*, Vol. 50, No 2, pp. 175-183.

Statistics Canada (2016), *Aboriginal Peoples in Canada: First Nations People, Métis and Inuit*, www12.statcan.gc.ca/nhs-enm/2011/as-sa/99-011-x/99-011-x2011001-eng.cfm.

Statistics New Zealand (2015), *Ethnic groups*, www.stats.govt.nz/browse_for_stats/ snapshots-of-nz/nz-in-profile-2015/about-new-zealand.aspx.

United Nations (2015), *Transforming our World: the 2030 Agenda for Sustainable Development*, https://sustainabledevelopment.un.org/post2015/transformingourworld.

UNESCO (1996), *Learning: The Treasure Within*, Report to UNESCO of the International Commission on Education for the Twenty-first Century (The Delors Report), UNESCO, Paris, www.unesco.org/new/en/education/themes/leading-the-international-agenda/rethinking-education/resources/.

Chapter 3

Indigenous peoples and education in participating Canadian provinces and territories

Colonisation processes have had a profoundly negative impact on successive generations of Indigenous peoples in Canada. UNICEF recently looked at four measures of child well-being: income inequality, educational inequality, health inequality and life satisfaction. Out of 35 countries, Canada ranks in 26th place, meaning that young Canadians grow up in contexts characterised by relatively wide inequalities, especially of income, health and life satisfaction, although less so for education. Indigenous populations account for a growing share of the population and of school students in Canada, and they tend to be younger than the non-Indigenous population. Canadian data show that poverty rates among the children of Indigenous families are higher than among non-Indigenous families. However, there are important differences in Indigenous populations, including size, languages, and approaches to identification/self-identification. This chapter presents basic demographic and economic data for each of the Canadian provinces and territories participating in this study, as well as facts relating to education and Indigenous populations. The participating provinces and territories are: Alberta, Manitoba, New Brunswick, Nova Scotia, Northwest Territories and Yukon.

This chapter sets out some broad context for the detailed analysis and discussion in the chapters that follow. The Indigenous populations covered in this study share crucial historical, cultural, and socio-economic characteristics, and yet each community is unique and specific. What they all share is a highly problematic and damaging history, epitomised in Canada's residential school system. It was only finally eradicated in the past twenty years, but its effects are ever-present. The trauma associated with that system came up repeatedly during our visits, with some proposing that its effects have actually become more manifest in passing from one generation to the next.

In this chapter, we do not seek to cover these effects in any detail. According to Dreise and Perrett (forthcoming): "... these issues are extensively rehearsed and analysed in each of the jurisdictions and include ongoing legacies of colonisation; the stain of racism; struggles associated with poverty; the battle to promote Indigenous 'voice' within dominant societies and institutions; and tensions that go to competing priorities and expectations between cultures." The issues do, however, provide the vital backdrop to and context of this report.

The chapter includes findings from studies by the OECD and UNICEF that place the countries in a wider international context regarding children, well-being and poverty. It then briefly considers the situation of the Indigenous populations in Canada in particular, before taking a more detailed look at the Canadian provinces and territories that participated in this study, providing some basic demographic and economic data for each of them, as well as facts relating to their education systems and their Indigenous populations.

International studies of well-being and child poverty

The OECD's most recent *How's Life?* study (OECD, 2015) provides the latest international evidence on well-being, including changes over time and inequalities in well-being outcomes among different groups, including age groups. Intergenerational inequalities can be stark. The steep increase in long-term unemployment that has occurred since 2009 has disproportionately affected young people.

Canada and Australia stand out as being among the countries with the highest mean levels of wealth (Australia, Canada, Luxembourg, Spain, the United Kingdom and the United States). The backdrop to the situation of Indigenous populations in the study locations is that these are particularly affluent countries. Canada is one of the countries where income and wealth are correlated the most closely, for rich and poor alike: "The correlation between income and wealth at the top end of the distribution is largest in Canada, Germany and Luxembourg, while at the bottom end it is largest in Canada, France, Italy and the United States" (OECD, 2015). So the context in Canada is one in which those who earn a lot are richer and those who earn least are poorer, relative to the majority of the more prosperous countries in the world.

How's Life? also charts the extent to which some children are getting a better start in life than others. Income poverty affects one child in seven in OECD countries, while 10% of children live in jobless households. Since the economic crisis, child poverty rates have risen in two-thirds of OECD countries and, in most, the poverty rate for children is higher than for the population in general (Figure 3.1). Looking at child well-being for the first time, the report shows how children from more affluent backgrounds tend to have better health and a happier school life. The report also shows that Canada and New Zealand were slightly above the OECD average for child poverty rates in 2011, compared to

Australia which is slightly below. In Canada and Australia, these rates had fallen slightly pre-crisis and post-crisis, while New Zealand has followed the majority international trend, with rising child poverty rates.

Figure 3.1. Percentage of children living in households earning 50% or less of median income

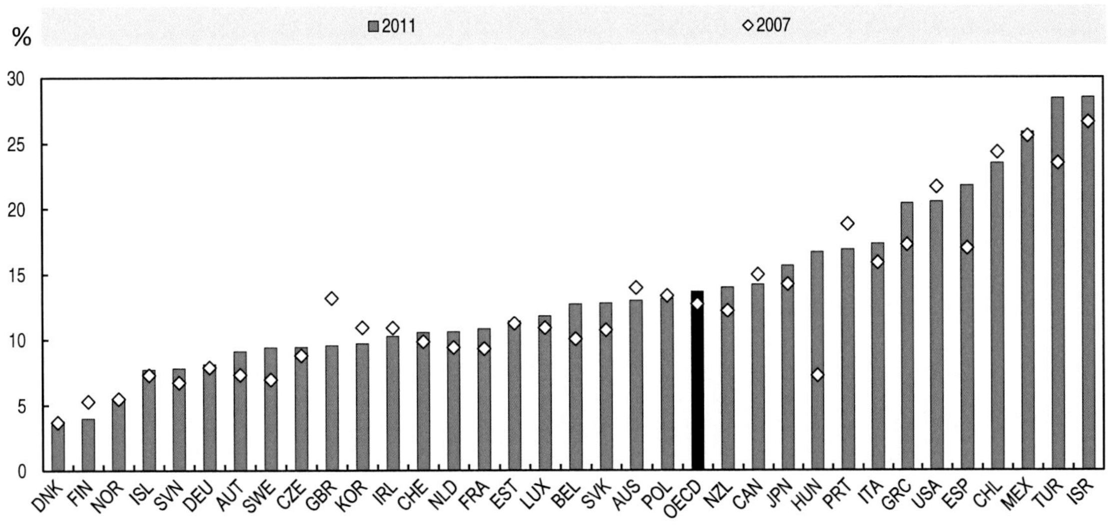

Note: The latest available year is 2012 for Australia, Hungary, Mexico and the Netherlands; 2010 for Belgium and 2009 for Japan.
Source: OECD (2015), *How's Life? 2015: Measuring Well-being*, http://dx.doi.org/10.1787/how_life-2015-en.

UNICEF (2016) also recently conducted an international study of child well-being, examining the situation in 35 countries (of which 31 are OECD countries, including Australia but not New Zealand). This study is not specifically related to Indigenous young people, but it ranks the countries included on four measures: income inequality, educational inequality, health inequality and life satisfaction.

Denmark, Finland, Norway and Switzerland come out as most equal when the four indices are aggregated, and Italy, Bulgaria, Turkey and Israel are the most unequal of the 35 countries. Canada comes well down the ranking, in 26th place, meaning that Canadian young people grow up in contexts that are characterised by marked inequalities compared with many other countries. This is especially the case as regards income, health and life satisfaction, but less so for education. Indigenous young people in Canada therefore live in communities and a society with significant inequalities on a range of measures that directly reflect their well-being.

Indigenous poverty rates in Canada

These general comparisons of child well-being place Canada in a situation with a relatively high level of inequalities. Key dimensions of those inequalities are income and poverty. A recent study analysing the 2011 Canadian National Household Survey data was able to distinguish between the different population groups: "This study uses the After Tax Low Income Measure (LIM-AT) following the convention of the OECD in determining 'low income'… the LIM-AT line is calculated as half of the median adjusted household income of the population" (Macdonald and Wilson, 2016, p.30). The study suggests that that child poverty rates stood at just over half (51%) for status First Nations children in 2010. They were higher still (60%) for those living on reserve, a figure that worsened from 2005, "with shocking rates of 76% in Manitoba and 69% in

Saskatchewan, easily the worst in the country" (p.6). By contrast, poverty rates among Indigenous children living off reserve have improved somewhat, while non-Indigenous children have seen little change to their circumstances since 2005. The highest poverty rates are thus among status First Nation children.

> A second tier encompasses other Indigenous children and disadvantaged groups. The children of immigrants in Canada suffer a child poverty rate of 32% ... Between these are found non-status First Nations children (30%), Inuit children (25%) and Métis children (23%). The third tier of poverty consists of children who are non-Indigenous, non-racialised and non-immigrant, where the rate of 13% is similar to the average among all countries [in the OECD]. (Macdonald and Wilson, 2016, p.5)

Essential context to the situation of the Indigenous children and young people in Canada is thus their clearly disadvantaged economic and material circumstances, although this also varies by Indigenous population and by province.

Indigenous populations in Canada and their education

The stark context of the situation of the Indigenous peoples in Canada is summarised in the very first paragraph of the Introduction to the Summary Report of the Truth and Reconciliation Commission published in 2015 (Honouring the Truth, Reconciling for the Future: Summary of the Final Report of the Truth and Reconciliation Commission of Canada):

> For over a century, the central goals of Canada's Aboriginal policy were to eliminate Aboriginal governments; ignore Aboriginal rights; terminate the Treaties; and, through a process of assimilation, cause Aboriginal peoples to cease to exist as distinct legal, social, cultural, religious, and racial entities in Canada. The establishment and operation of residential schools were a central element of this policy, which can best be described as "cultural genocide." (Truth and Reconciliation Commission of Canada, 2015a, p.1)

At least 150 000 First Nation, Métis, and Inuit students passed through residential schools in Canada. They were run by church denominations (mainly Roman Catholic, Anglican, United, Methodist and Presbyterian), and the government's partnership with them remained in place until the late 1960s. Most of these schools had closed by the 1980s, although the last federally-supported residential schools remained in operation until the late 1990s. Many references were made to us about the residential schools and the trauma they brought to Indigenous peoples. We heard too that this trauma continues, as the system has had profound intergenerational and community effects.

At the federal level, Prime Minister Trudeau pledged on taking office in 2015 that his government would immediately move to implement all 94 Calls to Action of the Truth and Reconciliation Commission, as well as to make new investments in First Nations education and to enter into detailed negotiations with Indigenous peoples. Those Calls to Action include the following basic equalising measures to address different attainment and funding gaps (Truth and Reconciliation Commission of Canada, 2015b):

- We call upon the federal, provincial, and territorial governments, in consultation and collaboration with Survivors, Aboriginal peoples, and educators, to:
  - Make age-appropriate curriculum on residential schools, Treaties, and Aboriginal peoples' historical and contemporary contributions to Canada a mandatory education requirement for Kindergarten to Grade Twelve students.

- Provide the necessary funding to post-secondary institutions to educate teachers on how to integrate Indigenous knowledge and teaching methods into classrooms.

- Provide the necessary funding to Aboriginal schools to utilise Indigenous knowledge and teaching methods in classrooms.

- Establish senior-level positions in government at the assistant deputy minister level or higher dedicated to Aboriginal content in education.

- We call upon the Council of Ministers of Education, Canada to maintain an annual commitment to Aboriginal education issues, including:

  - Developing and implementing Kindergarten to Grade Twelve curriculum and learning resources on Aboriginal peoples in Canadian history, and the history and legacy of residential schools.

  - Sharing information and best practices on teaching curriculum related to residential schools and Aboriginal history.

  - Building student capacity for intercultural understanding, empathy, and mutual respect.

  - Identifying teacher-training needs relating to the above.

An important contextual pattern for this study is demographic. Close to half (46%) of Indigenous people in Canada in 2011 were under the age of 25, compared with 30% of the non-Indigenous population (Kelly-Scott and Smith, 2015). The median age of First Nations people was nearly 26 years, while for Métis it was 31.4 years, and for Inuit, it was the lowest of the three, at just under 23 years. By contrast, the median age of the non-Indigenous population was 40.6 years. The Indigenous population is thus growing more quickly than the population in general, and Indigenous students make up a growing presence among those of school age. Well over a quarter of the Indigenous population (28%) are under age 15, compared with 16.5% in the non-Indigenous population (Statistics Canada, 2013).

A further critical context for this study is the fact that education policy is fundamentally a provincial and territorial responsibility, while the responsibility for schooling on reserves lies with the Indigenous peoples and the federal government. This report refers exclusively to education for Indigenous students in the provincial and territorial systems.

The Aboriginal Peoples Survey, 2012 (Statistics Canada, 2012) showed that 72% of First Nations people living off reserve, 42% of Inuit and 77% of Métis age 18 to 44 had a high school diploma or equivalent. In comparison, the 2011 National Household Survey revealed that 89% of the non-Indigenous population had at least a high school diploma (Statistics Canada, 2013). There has been rising attainment in general, but not all Indigenous populations have followed the same trajectory. According to Gordon and White (2014): "One may expect that over the past 15 years, the percentages of high school non-completions would decline and postsecondary attainment would increase … This trend was observed for Métis, off-reserve, non-status, and First Nations peoples.[1] These particular Indigenous groups have continuously had higher PSE [post-secondary education] attainment compared to Indigenous peoples living on reserve, status Indians, or Inuit peoples …". We can expect that these patterns reflect mobility patterns as well as the chances of people living on reserves to complete post-secondary education.

The participating Canadian systems

Figure 3.2. Total and Indigenous 2-18 year-olds in participating jurisdictions, 2015

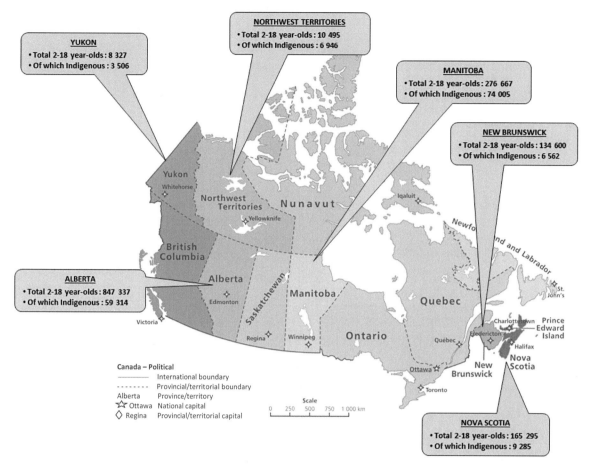

Sources:

For data: OECD calculations based on Statistics Canada's database (2011) and population growth estimate between 2011 and 2015.

For map: Wikipedia (2017), political map of Canada, https://en.wikipedia.org/wiki/File:Political_map_of_Canada.png. This work has been released into the public domain by its author, E Pluribus Anthony at the English Wikipedia project. This applies worldwide.

While there are broadly shared historical, social and demographic characteristics apparent across the different jurisdictions, the situation of Indigenous peoples across the country is far from identical. There are important variations in history and culture, and many languages (although they all share the fragility of Indigenous languages in face of globalising tendencies that are reducing the number of languages around the world). Looking at just two of the Canadian provinces in this study, in Alberta, there are 48 First Nations in three treaty areas and 8 Métis settlements, and in Manitoba, there are 63 First Nations, including 6 of the 20 largest bands in Canada. There are also very wide differences within Indigenous populations as to whether their context and residential environment is urban, rural or remote.

Alberta

Alberta has the second-highest gross domestic product (GDP) per capita in Canada, although it is now facing the problems of low oil prices. The total population of Alberta in 2015 was 4.2 million or 11% of the total Canadian population. Alberta's population growth was the second-highest among the Canadian jurisdictions, comparing census data for 2015 with 2006-11 (11%, compared to Canadian average of 5%). As elsewhere, population growth is notably higher among the Indigenous population.

By law, children living in Alberta must attend school from age 6 to age 16. The school system is divided into kindergarten (K), elementary (Grades 1-6), junior high (Grades 7-9) and high school (Grades 10-12). In Alberta, there are 1 498 public schools and 391 separate schools (mainly Catholic) that provide offer education in English, as well as 40 francophone schools. Around 90% of students in the province attend one of these three school types, which are funded by the province and governed by publicly-elected school boards. There are also charter schools and private schools, as well as band-operated schools, which are not included in this study.

There were just over 220 000 people reporting Indigenous identity in Alberta in 2011, which was nearly 16% of Canada's total Indigenous population in 2011 (Statistics Canada, 2013). Indigenous students in Alberta are identified through voluntary self-identification on school registration forms, with students and parents given the opportunity annually to change or remove this identifier. In the 2014/15 school year, there were just over 676 000 students enrolled in provincial K-12 education (including those living on reserves), of which approximately 7% identified as Indigenous.

Over a quarter of Indigenous people (28%) in Alberta reside in Edmonton, and one in seven (15%) in Calgary, although these represent only 5% of the population of Edmonton and 3% of the population of Calgary. There are 48 First Nations in three treaty areas. The most commonly spoken First Nations languages are Blackfoot, Cree, Chipewyan, Dene, Sarcee and Stoney (Nakoda Sioux). There are also eight Métis settlements in Alberta, the only land-based Métis in Canada, where the Michif language is spoken. According to the Aboriginal Peoples Survey, 2012 (Statistics Canada, 2012), nearly half of the Indigenous people in Alberta aged 25 to 64 had a certificate, diploma or degree from a trade school, college or university, 40% of First Nations people, 53% of Métis and 52% of Inuit (compared to 65% for their non- Indigenous counterparts).

Manitoba

Manitoba has the sixth-highest GDP per capita in Canada, although, according to the Conference Board of Canada (2015b), it is poised to become one of Canada's leaders in economic growth because of the key sectors of construction, manufacturing and service industries. By law, children living in Manitoba must attend school from age 7 to age 18, but 6-year-olds have the right to attend school. The school system is divided into early years (K-4), middle years (Grades 5-8), and high school (Grades 9-12). In 2015/16, there were approximately 183 000 students enrolled from K-12. There are 37 school divisions and 691 public schools, that provide education in English, as well as 24 francophone schools.

The total population of Manitoba in 2011 was just over 1.2 million (0.3 % of the total Canadian population). Nearly 196 000 people self-identified as Indigenous in the National Household Survey, 2011 (Statistics Canada, 2013). Four in ten Indigenous people in Manitoba reside in Winnipeg, representing 11% of the total population of the city. Indigenous people make up more than one-third of the total population of Thompson (35%) and nearly one-quarter (23%) of Portage la Prairie. Manitoba has 63 First Nations, including 6 of the 20 largest bands in Canada. There are seven main linguistic groups: Anishinaabe (Ojibway), Cree, Dakota, Dene, Michif, Oji-Cree and Inuktitut. There are seven treaties with First Nations in the province, although five Manitoba First Nations are not signatory to any treaty with Canada (Birdtail Sioux, Sioux Valley, Canupawakpa, Dakota Tipi and Dakota Plains).

In 2011, 40% of the Indigenous people in Manitoba aged 25 to 64 had a certificate, diploma or degree from a trade school, college or university: 31% of First Nations people, 49% of Métis and 40% of Inuit (compared to 60% for their non-Indigenous counterparts) There was also a difference in the proportion of Indigenous and non-Indigenous people with no certificate, diploma or degree. In 2011, 50% of First Nations people aged 25-64, 24% of Métis and 27% of Inuit did not have a certificate, diploma or degree (compared to 14% for the non-Indigenous population).

New Brunswick

New Brunswick has the second lowest GDP per capita in Canada and was among the slower-growing provincial economies in 2016. Its population density is much higher than the Canadian average, but its population growth is significantly lower. The provincially-funded public education system, kindergarten to Grade 12, is offered through a dual system of English and French schools. Attendance at New Brunswick public schools is compulsory until the completion of high school or age 18. The school system is divided into kindergarten, elementary (Grades K-5), middle school (Grades 6-8) and high school (Grades 9-12).

The total population of New Brunswick in 2011 was a little over 750 000 of which just over 22 600 people self-identified as Indigenous in the National Household Survey, 2011 (Statistics Canada, 2013). One in seven (15%) Indigenous people in the province live in Fredericton, making up around 4% of the city's total population. A further 11% reside in Saint John and Moncton, making up 2% of the total population in both cities. In New Brunswick, there are 15 First Nations, of which 9 are Mi'kmaq and 6 are Maliseet (Wolastoqey). The languages most spoken in the province are English and French, followed by Mi'kmaq.

There are seven school districts in New Brunswick, of which four are English-speaking (with total enrolment of Indigenous students of 1 454) and three are francophone, with low enrolment of Indigenous students (72). In 2008, the New Brunswick Department of Education, Indian and Northern Affairs Canada and the Indigenous Affairs Secretariat, signed a Memorandum of Understanding (MOU) with 14 of the 15 First Nation communities in the province. The MOU signified the desire of all parties to work together towards improving the educational outcomes of First Nations students. According to the Aboriginal Peoples Survey, 2012 (Statistics Canada, 2012), 51% of Indigenous people in New Brunswick aged 25 to 64 have a certificate, diploma or degree from a trade school, college or university (compared to 57% of their non-Indigenous counterparts).

Northwest Territories

The total population of the Northwest Territories in 2011 was 41 462 (less than one percent). Between 2006 and 2011 in the Northwest Territories, there was little or no population growth, compared to the average of 5% for Canada as a whole. The communities in the Northwest Territories range in size from the capital city of Yellowknife, with a population of just over 19 000, to the community of Jean Marie River with a population of 71 people. Each community has its own school. The Northwest Territories has the highest GDP per capita in Canada, but according to the Conference Board of Canada (2015a), difficulties are associated with falling oil prices.

By law, children living in the Northwest Territories must attend school from age 6 to age 16. The school system is divided into kindergarten, elementary (Grades 1-6), junior high (Grades 7-9) and high school (Grades 10-12). There are eight education jurisdictions within the Northwest Territories. Each region is represented by either a Divisional Education Council (DEC) or a school board. The superintendent is the representative of the employer in each DEC or school board. There are 49 schools in the territory.

The first inhabitants of today's Northwest Territories were the Dene. Ancestors of today's Dene were small bands of hunters who followed migrating caribou and other animals into areas near Great Slave Lake, Great Bear Lake and along the Mackenzie River. Today, there are a number of tribal groupings within the larger Dene group: the Chipewyan, Tlicho, Yellowknives, South Slavey, North Slavey, Gwich'in and Sahtu Dene. There are 11 official languages in the Northwest Territories: Chipewyan, Cree, English, French, Gwich'in, Inuinnaqtun, Inuktitut, Inuvialuktun, North Slavey, South Slavey and Tlicho.

Of the total population of just under 42 000, just over half self-identified as Indigenous in the National Household Survey, 2011 (Statistics Canada, 2013). In 2005, one in four Indigenous people in the Northwest Territories resided in an urban area, and more than one in ten (15%) in a rural area, so that the majority are in remote areas.

Nova Scotia

Nova Scotia's population in 2011 was nearly 922 000 (3% of the total Canadian population). It had the third-lowest GDP per capita in Canada, but the prognosis of the Conference Board of Canada (2015a) is for increasing growth. Nova Scotia has relatively slow population growth, 0.9% compared to 5.9% in Canada as a whole. The largest metropolitan area is Halifax (population of 390 000), followed by Cape Breton (101 000). The most spoken languages in the province, according to the 2011 census, are English, French, Arabic, Algonquian and Mi'kmaq languages. By law, children living in Nova Scotia must attend school from age 5 to age 16. In the 2014/15 school year, there were 118 152 students enrolled in K-12 education. Nova Scotia has seven English-language school boards and one French-language school board.

Approximately 2% of the Indigenous-identity population in Canada, nearly 34 000, lived in Nova Scotia in 2011. Three in ten (29%) Indigenous people in Nova Scotia reside in Halifax, representing 3% of the total population of the city, while Cape Breton had the province's highest proportion of Indigenous people, at 6%. The Mi'kmaq are the founding people of Nova Scotia and remain the predominant Indigenous group. There are 13 Mi'kmaq First Nations in the province, with community populations ranging from 283 in the Annapolis Valley First Nation to 4 314 in the Eskasoni First Nation. The Registered Indian population in Nova Scotia is represented through a series of 13 band councils and 2 tribal councils, the Confederacy of Mainland Mi'kmaq and the Union of Nova Scotia Indians. Mi'kmaw Kina'matnewey, the on-reserve education authority in Nova Scotia for 12 of the 13 band councils, is a unique example of First Nation self-governance in the area of education. There is both federal and provincial legislation giving full authority to lead education on-reserve to the 12 band council Chiefs and through ongoing dialogue and relationship building, Mi'kmaw Kina'matnewey works with provincial Department of Education and Early Childhood Development and strives for seamless transitions for students between First Nation schools and the public school system. The partnership between Mi'kmaw Kina'matnewey and the Department is critical as not all band councils have schools on-reserve and they rely extensively on the public school system to provide an equitable education.

In 2011, 59% of Indigenous people in Nova Scotia aged 25 to 64 had a certificate, diploma or degree from a trade school, college or university: 56% of First Nations people, 66% of Métis and 68% of Inuit (compared to 64% for their non-Indigenous counterparts), and 21% of First Nations people aged 25 to 64, 16% of Métis and 17% of Inuit did not have a certificate, diploma or degree in 2011.

Yukon

Yukon has the third highest GDP per capita in Canada, with mining developments expected to push growth higher. Yukon has the highest population growth among all Canadian jurisdictions, at 11.6%, compared to 5.9% in Canada as a whole. Yukon children must attend school from age 6 years and 8 months (on September 1) until at least age 16, except by special arrangement (Yukon Legislative Council Office, 2016).

The school system is mainly divided into kindergarten, elementary school (Grades 1-7), and secondary school (Grades 8-12). This differs for the French-language schools and in some rural areas where, for example, students may complete all grades at the same school, or they may have to complete the final high school grades in Whitehorse or through online or distance learning. There are 28 schools in the territory, with 14 located in Whitehorse and 14 in the rural communities. Enrolments in the schools range from fewer than 10 students to over 600 students, with a total enrolment of just over 5 200 students in September 2014.

The total population of Yukon in 2011 was just under 34 000 (less than 1% of the total Canadian population), of which 7 705 self-identified as Indigenous in the National Household Survey, 2011 (Statistics Canada, 2013). At the time of 2006 census, about one-third of the Indigenous population in Yukon lived in urban areas. There are 14 First Nations in Yukon, 11 with settled land claims with the Government of Yukon and Canada. The most spoken languages in the province are English, French, German and Athapaskan. In the 2014/15 school year, there were 5 243 students enrolled in 28 K-12 schools, of which 1 578 self-identified as Indigenous (31% of the total student population). There are gaps in attendance and student achievement between Indigenous and non-Indigenous students, and also between rural and urban students.

Note

1. As noted in the article, First Nations persons can be either "status" or "non-status". Given that non-status Indians have higher educational attainment, the mean levels of the First Nation category are inflated.

References

Conference Board of Canada (2015a), "Economic Outlook for the Territories in 2015 is Encouraging", Conference Board of Canada, Ottawa, www.conferenceboard. ca/press/newsrelease/14-12-16/economic_outlook_for_the_territories_in_2015_is_ encouraging.aspx.

Conference Board of Canada (2015b), "Manitoba's Economy Will Continue to Flourish in 2016", Conference Board of Canada, Ottawa, www.conferenceboard.ca/press/ newsrelease/15-12-07/manitoba_s_economy_will_continue_to_flourish_in_2016.aspx.

Gordon, C.E. and J.P White (2014), "Indigenous Educational Attainment in Canada", *The International Indigenous Policy Journal*, 5(3), http://ir.lib.uwo.ca/iipj/vol5/iss3/6.

Kelly-Scott, K. and K. Smith (2015), "Aboriginal peoples: Fact sheet for Canada", Statistics Canada, Ottawa, www.statcan.gc.ca/pub/89-656-x/89-656-x2015001-eng.pdf.

Macdonald, D. and D. Wilson (2016), "Shameful Neglect: Indigenous Child Poverty in Canada", Canadian Centre for Policy Alternatives, Ottawa, www.policyalternatives. ca/publications/reports/shameful-neglect.

Northwest Territories Teachers' Association (2016), "Divisional Education Councils and School Boards", Northwest Territories Teachers' Association, Yellowknife, www.nwtta.nt.ca/en/Collective_Agreements_27/Divisional_Education_CouncilsScho ol_Boards_-_Contact_Information_366.html.

OECD (2015), *How's Life? 2015: Measuring Well-being*, OECD Publishing, Paris, http://dx.doi.org/10.1787/how_life-2015-en.

Statistics Canada (2013), "Aboriginal Peoples in Canada: First Nations People, Métis and Inuit", National Household Survey, 2011, Statistics Canada, Ottawa, www12.statcan.gc.ca/nhs-enm/2011/as-sa/99-011-x/99-011-x2011001-eng.pdf.

Statistics Canada (2012), "Aboriginal Peoples Survey", Statistics Canada, Ottawa, www5.statcan.gc.ca/olc-cel/olc.action?objId=89-653-X&objType=2&lang=en& limit=0.

Truth and Reconciliation Commission of Canada (2015a), "Honouring the Truth, Reconciling for the Future: Summary of the Final Report of the Truth and Reconciliation Commission of Canada", www.trc.ca/websites/trcinstitution/File/ 2015/Findings/Exec_Summary_2015_05_31_web_o.pdf.

Truth and Reconciliation Commission of Canada (2015b), "Truth and Reconciliation Commission of Canada: Calls to Action", Truth and Reconciliation Commission of Canada, Winnipeg, www.trc.ca/websites/trcinstitution/File/2015/Findings/Calls_to_ Action_English2.pdf.

UNICEF Office of Research (2016) "Fairness for Children: A league table of inequality in child well-being in rich countries", Innocenti Report Card 13, UNICEF Office of Research – Innocenti, Florence, www.unicef.pt/RC13_Equidade_para_as_criancas.pdf.

Yukon Legislative Council Office (2016), "Education Act, Section 22", Legislative Counsel Office, Whitehorse, www.gov.yk.ca/legislation/acts/education_c.pdf.

Chapter 4

Improving the well-being of Indigenous young people

Well-being is central to approaches to Indigenous education and Indigenous values. Five dimensions usefully define well-being in young people: cognitive, psychological, physical, social and material. This chapter focuses especially on the social, psychological and physical dimensions. A number of indicators give rise to concern about the well-being of Indigenous young people, although data are inadequate to build a full picture. But there are also promising signs that trends are improving and that the differences between Indigenous and non-Indigenous students are relatively small. There is concern about low levels of trust and confidence in the education system among Indigenous parents. Recognition of culture, language and identity is an integral part of well-being, but it is difficult to recruit adequate staff and trained Indigenous teachers. However, the promotion of Indigenous culture and identity has implications for the professional development and practice of all educators. Building trust is even more essential because of the historical context of residential schools and colonialism, as well as the privileged place of relationships in Indigenous cultures. Land-based programmes represent examples of project-based learning, community engagement, and a sustainability focus that are lessons for good practice everywhere, not only for Indigenous students.

The concept of well-being is a central one in this review. It features prominently in contemporary policy discourse and in approaches related to Indigenous education and to beliefs and value systems of Indigenous peoples. Well-being is multidimensional and thus widens concepts of success, achievement and effectiveness beyond measurable educational outcomes, such as attainment and achievement, just as the wider concept of well-being informs OECD policy criteria beyond single economic measures such as GDP. The different dimensions that contribute to well-being may be seen as both components of it and objectives to be addressed. The different dimensions are also interconnected, each influencing the others.

The OECD framework for measuring well-being (across all sectors, not just education) is reproduced below (Figure 4.1), and all its dimensions are relevant to this chapter. The multidimensionality of well-being can be positive in that it is more comprehensive than single measures, but it may be negative if it results in approaches that become fragmented into multiple but unconnected components, rather than the holistic approach intended.

Well-being, children and young people

Well-being features increasingly in OECD's work on children, young people and education. It has been conceptualised and informs the OECD Programme for International Student Assessment (PISA) 2015 (Borgonovi and Pál, 2016). Five dimensions of students' well-being are captured, and these align closely with definitions in other studies and with the coverage in this report.

For PISA 2015, well-being covers:

- *Cognitive well-being*, the skills and foundations students need to participate effectively in today's society, as lifelong learners, effective workers and engaged citizens (Pollard and Lee, 2003).

- Psychological well-being, which includes the views of young people about their lives, their engagement with school, and their goals and ambitions for the future.

- Physical well-being, referring to health status and engagement in healthy activities and eating habits (Statham and Chase, 2010).

- Social well-being, the quality of the social lives of young people (Rath, Harter and Harter, 2010), including relationships with family, peers and school life (Pollard and Lee, 2003).

- Material well-being, as material resources allow families to better provide for children's needs and schools to support learning and healthy development; children who live in poverty are more likely to have health problems (Aber et al., 1997), perform poorly in school (OECD, 2013), and earn less later in life (Case, Fertig and Paxson, 2005).

Figure 4.1. Individual well-being and sustainability over time

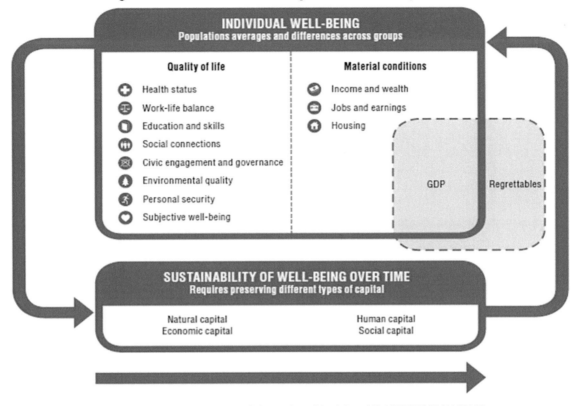

Source: OECD (2011), *How's Life?: Measuring Well-being*, http://dx.doi.org/10.1787/9789264121164-en.

The literature review prepared for this project (Dreise and Perrett, forthcoming) refers to an earlier mapping of well-being (Fraillon, 2004), which included very similar dimensions to those of the OECD/PISA study. Fraillon defines it as follows:

> Well-being is the state of successful performance throughout the life course integrating physical, cognitive, and social-emotional functions that results in productive activities deemed significant by one's cultural community, fulfilling social relationships, and the ability to transcend moderate psychosocial and environmental problems. Well-being also has a subjective dimension in the sense of satisfaction associated with fulfilling one's potential. (p.20)

Fraillon identifies five dimensions and describes qualities that students will ideally possess within the intrapersonal dimension:

Dimensions	Qualities
1. Physical	Autonomy Emotional regulation
2. Economic	Resilience Self-efficacy
3. Psychological (intrapersonal)	Self-esteem Spirituality
4. Cognitive	Curiosity Engagement
5. Social (interpersonal)	Mastery orientation

This chapter deals primarily with policies and practices related to the social, psychological and physical dimensions, as included in both the OECD/PISA list and the Fraillon list. The economic dimension was discussed in the previous chapter, while the cognitive and educational components are the focus of subsequent chapters.

However, while this schema provides a useful universal umbrella within which to understand well-being, we have already noted above that a key issue is how far the concept of well-being in practice serves to integrate rather than lead to fragmentation. There is also the question of how social it is understood to be, as opposed to so many traits attaching to individuals. In our view, while the measurement of well-being might often rely on charting characteristics of individuals, well-being understood in this multidimensional way is fundamentally about relationships and the nature of social relations.

Indigenous definitions of well-being

The above definitions of well-being are universal in scope but we should recognise that there is not a single Indigenous definition that might inform policies and practices. Such definitions as there are coalesce around the holistic. Dreise and Perrett (forthcoming) refer to the work of Ritchie et al. (2014) in their discussion of what constitutes well-being among Indigenous peoples in Canada, seeing it as combining the physical (body), mental (mind), emotional (heart) and spiritual (spirit), "a holistic view of health that is in harmony with the individual, the community, and the natural World". In Australia, similar holistic definitions of well-being exist. Nguyen and Cairney (2013) propose connection to land and country as key in promoting holistic well-being (physical, social, emotional, cultural and spiritual). They find that for Aboriginal and Torres Strait Islander people, involvement in managing country can result in confirmation of identity and cultural authority; social activities; building and maintaining relationships; provision of purpose; traditional education; and sharing knowledge, exercise and food.

Haswell et al. (2013) explain that the term "social and emotional well-being" has a very specific set of meanings to Aboriginal and Torres Strait Islander peoples. It is fundamental to health and embedded, with culture, in the way that health is defined. They stress that it extends beyond the aggregated well-being of individuals to more social definitions, embracing "the social, emotional and cultural well-being of the whole community" (p.23). This helps to shift the focus away from traits attaching to individuals and to look for well-being in the strength, vitality and sustainability of communities. The Māori perspective of well-being, the *Whare Tapa Whā* model, is used especially in health and social services and makes explicit spiritual well-being. Māori expert Mason Durie developed this model in 1982 to reflect the Māori view of health and wellness around four dimensions: *taha wairua* (spiritual health), *taha hinengaro* (mental health), *taha tinana* (physical health) and *taha whānau* (family health). Different parts of a *wharenui* (meeting house) represent each of these dimensions.

The sections that follow describe the findings of the latest Canadian Health Behaviour in School-Aged Children (HBSC) study on well-being, against which specific findings and promising practices can be put in context (Freeman, King and Pickett, 2016). This is a major international survey, the most recent round of which took place in 2014, with results reported in 2016.

Holistic and multidimensional approaches

It follows from the multidimensional nature of well-being, and from the multifaceted nature of education and society, that many of the most effective strategies embrace different dimensions at the same time. Doyle and Hill (2008) highlight the importance of holistic schooling approaches and a student support services model through culturally and contextually relevant learning. Such approaches require meeting the needs of the whole child, including health, nutrition, transportation and intensive academic support where required. Mulford (2011) stresses the similarity of conclusions from research on teacher quality and sustainability and recommended policy and practice in Indigenous education, including self-determination, increased individual and collective capacity building, culturally relevant and context-specific education practices, and working together through partnerships, networks and shared leadership. Dreise and Thomson (2014) refer to this at the level of the school or learning centre: "…high-performing schools are ones that take a wider lens to student well being" (p.4).

Therefore, some of the most interesting policies and practices addressing well-being are not specifically targeted at one or another of the dimensions of well-being for Indigenous populations, but at several dimensions at once. In Canada, many of these are recent. In New Zealand, on the other hand, the Treaty of Waitangi was signed in 1840 as a founding document of the country itself and so has had far longer to help define core values and practices. Among other things, it states: "Under this Treaty, responsibility for Māori language (and its revival) is shared between Māori and the Crown." There is also a clearly different context in Canada, where many treaties are being negotiated and signed, compared with a single core treaty arrangement.[1]

Hence, overarching commitments set frameworks to the specifically negotiated arrangements with each Indigenous population. Such important major steps and documents include the reports of the Truth and Reconciliation Commission of Canada (2015) or the United Nations Declaration on the Rights of Indigenous Peoples (UNDRIP). Among the participating provinces, for instance, it was only in July 2015 that the Government of Alberta announced its commitment to implement the objectives and principles of the UNDRIP – a reminder of how recent have been many of the steps and measures taken and the time that will be needed for them to embed.

Where systems develop overarching strategies and frameworks, it means they seek to ensure that the many different reforms and innovations taken add up to a coherent whole. Examples include the First Nation, Métis and Inuit Education Policy Framework, in place in Alberta since 2002, engaging consultations to set goals and performance measures around how Indigenous perspectives and languages are included in the curriculum. The Solid partners Solid futures strategy[2] in Queensland was the overarching departmental strategy on Indigenous education. The key principles were effective engagement and connections; working together better and smarter; cultural capability and recognition; supporting successful transitions; and building workforce and leadership capacity.

One general and promising approach is the establishment of platforms and data banks of relevant innovations and practices on which educators and community stakeholders can draw, rather than having to continually reinvent the wheel. One such resource is the Promising Practices for First Nations, Métis and Inuit Learner Success initiative in Alberta, which showcases schools with innovative practices that support Indigenous community engagement. It highlights examples of best practices, innovative collaboration models and community engagement strategies that benefit the entire student body.

Another general approach in Canada, that offers tools and resources for schools and communities to generate their own knowledge in order to advance, is the OurSCHOOL evaluation instrument (formerly called Tell Them from Me), designed to increase student outcomes, including well-being and safety. This surveys the well-being of young children in Canada and has become the largest survey tool in Canada since its inception in 2005. It may be used at the provincial level. For example, the 2013/14 Manitoba Provincial Report, entitled *Tell Them from Me: Bullying and School Safety*, was used to conclude that there is "an overall high prevalence in verbal, social, and physical bullying and lower prevalence in cyberbullying" (Manitoba Education and Advanced Learning, 2014). This has in turn shaped policy, and the province is partnering with organisations and providing resources to intervene with these trends. In Alberta, well-being surveys are done at the school level, and many schools use these to inform their approaches to Indigenous issues and students. Each year, Alberta Education produces report cards with 16 selected indicators for schools to use as a basis for an evaluative discussion.

Similarly, in New Zealand, *Rongohia te Hau* is a survey tool which makes it possible for schools to obtain a snapshot of how their Māori learners experience school: "*Rongohia te Hau* gives schools a picture of their pedagogy, asking how is teaching being done in this school. It co-constructs the process for understanding classroom practice across a school. The evidence that is gathered tells schools how they can change their pedagogy if they want to make more of a difference for their Māori students".[3] Note that this tool is optional, which means that no information is collected nationally, and the number of schools using it is unknown.

The Australian Curriculum mandates that Aboriginal and Torres Strait Islander histories and cultures are a cross-curriculum priority, such that Indigenous perspectives need to be embedded across the curriculum. They are also now embedded within the Australian Professional Standards for Teachers, which specify what teachers should know and can do in order to teach Aboriginal and Torres Strait Islander students and to teach Aboriginal and Torres Strait Islander languages, history and culture to all Australian students. The aim is to shift Indigenous perspectives from electives and the periphery to core business. In New Zealand, graduating teacher standards[4] include such specified competences as: 1) have content and pedagogical content knowledge for supporting English as an Additional Language or Dialect (EAL/D) learners to succeed in the curriculum; 2) have knowledge of *tikanga* and *te reo Māori* to work effectively within the bicultural contexts; 3) have an understanding of education within the New Zealand bicultural, multicultural, social, political, economic and historical contexts; and 4) demonstrate respect for *te reo Māori me ngā tikanga-ā-iwi* in their practice. This is supported by a practical tool called *Tātaiako*.[5]

The social dimension of well-being

In this section, we look more specifically at the social dimension of well-being. This is partly about the recognition of culture, values and ethnicity, as an important dimension of well-being is the experienced sense of inclusion and exclusion. The social dimension is partly about connection to family and community, and this in turn has both social and geographical dimensions, the latter especially relating to living distant from centres of population (including educational resources).

The recent HBSC survey from 2014 suggests that for young people in Canada as a whole, boys tend to be less socially connected than girls, except for sports (Freeman, King and Pickett, 2016). However, as will be seen later in this chapter, girls have higher reported levels of anxiety and problems regarding emotional well-being. For both boys and girls, there have been longer-term increases in a sense of distrust. About one in six students felt that most people in their neighbourhood would try to take advantage of them if they had the chance, and the percentage of students who felt distrust towards others increased between 2002 and 2014. Regardless of grade, boys consistently reported lower levels of friend support than girls and lower levels of involvement in community activities and groups, and they were less likely to say they were involved in volunteer work or arts groups. However, boys were more likely to report being involved in team sports (Gariépy et al., 2016).

Well-being among Māori and non-Māori students

New Zealand's most recent PISA survey data allow comparisons to be made between Māori and non-Māori 15-year-olds on a range of indicators relevant to well-being: sense of belonging to school, motivation to achieve, test anxiety, positive disposition towards co-operation, and reported sense of parental support. Figure 4.2 permits comparisons of Māori and non-Māori against the international averages on these dimensions, and also indicates where statistically significant differences are found between Māori and non-Māori young people.

Figure 4.2. Well-being scores of Māori and non-Māori students in 2015, compared with international averages

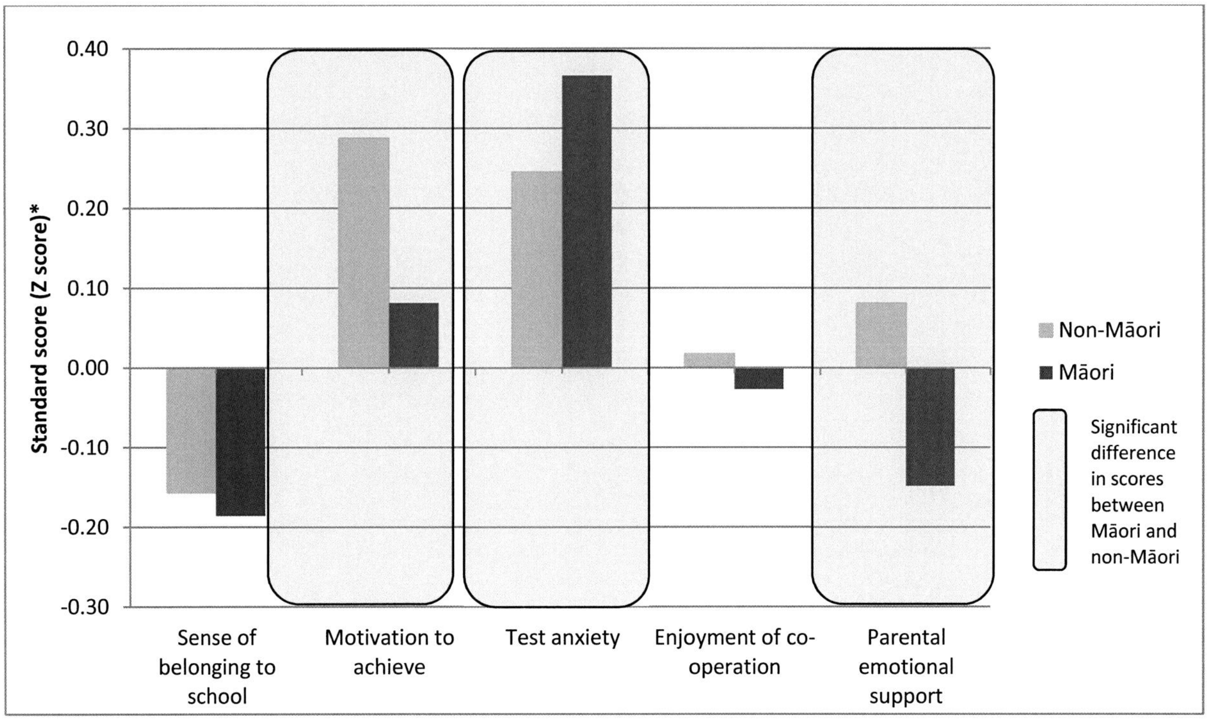

Note:*0 equals international average score.

Source: OECD (2016), PISA 2015 Database, www.oecd.org/pisa/data/2015database/.

Māori students feel a generally lower motivation to learn and greater test anxiety, and they perceive lower levels of parental support (Figure 4.2). Compared to international averages, New Zealand students, both Māori and non-Māori, report a lower sense of belonging to school and a greater sense of anxiety than 15-year-olds across OECD countries as a whole. On the more positive side, both Māori and non-Māori students have greater motivation to achieve than OECD 15-year-olds as a whole. So while the Māori students have lower motivation to achieve than New Zealand students as a whole, they have somewhat greater motivation than their peers in other countries.

Specific provincial findings

New Brunswick conducts a Student Wellness Survey, in which it can distinguish between Indigenous and non-Indigenous students. Some principal findings are presented below (Table 4.1).

Table 4.1. New Brunswick Student Wellness Survey results on student perceptions of support, Grades 6-12, 2012/13

Survey topic	Indigenous students (%)	Non-Indigenous students (%)	Gap between Indigenous and non-Indigenous students (%)
I know where to go in my community to get help.	23	26	-3
I have people I look up to.	40	47	-7
My parents/caregivers know a lot about me.	40	51	-11
My family stands by me during difficult times.	43	50	-7
My friends stand by me during difficult times.	40	46	-6
I am treated fairly in my community.	27	38	-11
I feel I belong at my school.	23	31	-8
I enjoy my culture and family traditions.	43	42	1

Source: New Brunswick Health Council (2013), www.nbhc.ca/surveys/nbsws#.WSMBE2996Uk.

Among Indigenous students, 40% have confidence that their parents/caregivers know them well, a gap of 10% compared to non-Indigenous students (51%). Relatively fewer Indigenous students say that they have someone to look up to, and similarly fewer feel that they can rely on family and friends to stand by them. Just over a quarter (27%) of Indigenous students feel that they are treated fairly in their community, compared to 38% of non-Indigenous students. At the same time a larger proportion, albeit still a minority, enjoy their culture and traditions, with a slight advantage in this case among Indigenous students. It is important to note not only the differences between Indigenous and non-Indigenous students' views, but the actual levels measured. These are cause for concern, as only around a quarter to a third of young people feel that they belong at school. These findings suggest that there is still a long way to go to establish high levels of trust and engagement.

In Alberta, within the Provincial Satisfaction Survey[6], Indigenous and non-Indigenous students and parents were asked about such matters as school inclusion/integration, safety, academic achievement, teaching quality, tolerance for cultural diversity, physical health regarding exercise and nutrition, community involvement and connectedness, social skills and career readiness and healthy relationships among peers and teachers regarding trust and respect. The positive aspects of these surveys are the generally high reported levels of satisfaction among students and the lack of significant differences between Indigenous and non-Indigenous students. On the other hand, parents of Indigenous students in Alberta indicate lower levels of satisfaction than either their children or non-Indigenous parents. Indigenous parents, it appears, are less convinced than their children that schools are performing well enough. This relates to issues of trust that are fundamental to developing the sense of connection and engagement that we discuss later in this report.

Among the provinces and territories participating in this study, the New Brunswick Student Wellness Survey found that the majority of Indigenous students (70%) consider education regarding their cultural heritage to be important. That is positive news. However, the survey also found that less than half of non- Indigenous students (47%) see education contributing to cultural heritage as being important.

Policies and practices on the social and cultural dimension of well-being

Research highlights the positive benefits of embracing culture in classrooms (Dreise and Perret, forthcoming). Successful schools provide environments where Indigenous students feel connected and valued. This can be achieved through the representation of Indigenous cultures in the classroom and celebrating them throughout the school programme. Practical steps can be taken, including making available Indigenous books and other resources and by embedding Indigenous perspectives in the curriculum and the life of schools. We saw a number of examples of this.

Language is clearly a key issue. The Mi'kmaw and Wolastoqey Language Curriculum in New Brunswick is a high school curriculum developed at different levels, and offered from Grades 9 to 12 through a mix of face-to-face and online activities. It is regarded as a vital part of the preservation and revitalisation of the language and culture of the 15 First Nation Communities in that province, and the language is taught within themes that resonate with those communities. The curriculum also includes traditional music, visual art and traditional stories.

Ka Hikitia - Accelerating Success, the national Māori education strategy in New Zealand, identifies learning of the Māori language as a priority focus across all levels of education. *Tau Mai Te Reo* for high-quality Māori language education in New Zealand schools is a national strategy to create the conditions for learners to enjoy and achieve education and Māori language outcomes, support the co-ordination of efforts in Māori language in across education agencies. It provides a framework for better government investment in Māori language in education. All parents in New Zealand can request that their school provide instruction for their children in the Māori language and culture. In New Zealand, Māori is recognised as an official language, and it has a special status within the curriculum in addition to being offered as a subject (Box 4.1).

Box 4.1. Strengthening identity, language and culture through education

Parents in New Zealand have the opportunity to enrol their children in range of government funded early childhood education and schooling options in the medium of the Māori language, where children are taught in and through the Māori language for at least 51% of their time.

Early learning Māori language immersion centres, are now an important part of New Zealand's early childhood education system. These were first established as *kōhanga reo* (language nests) in 1982. In June 2015, New Zealand had 450 Māori immersion early learning centres, the majority of which are *kōhanga reo*, provision serving around 9 000 children. This represents approximately 5% of all children attending early childhood education each year, or 22.5% of all Māori children.

Kōhanga reo were established through Māori community efforts and play a key role in the revitalisation of the Māori language. *Kōhanga reo* philosophies and practices reflect the important role of *whānau* (family) in the growth and development of children. The *kōhanga reo* concept was developed to provide the following benefits to children and their families and communities:

- ensure the survival and revival of the Māori language
- affirm the identity, language and culture of learners and their families
- immerse *kōhanga reo mokopuna* (children) and their families in the principles of Māori child rearing practices, through the medium of *te reo Māori me ona tīkanga* (customary practices)
- develop and upskill families.

During their schooling years, children can continue their Māori medium education in *kura* and *wharekura* (primary and secondary Māori medium schooling). The first *kura kaupapa Māori* opened in 1985 and since then, a nationwide network of Māori medium *kura* has developed. As with *kōhanga reo* they all began as Māori community initiatives to ensure that Māori language and Māori culture survived. Teaching and learning in Māori medium is guided by *Te Marautanga o Aotearoa (2008)*, which forms New Zealand's nationally mandated curriculum alongside the English medium *The New Zealand Curriculum (2007)*. *Te Marautanga o Aotearoa* outlines the core learning and competencies students will develop in Māori medium education, including the knowledge and skills to enter university and follow chosen careers; and the development of cultural knowledge and identity. Māori medium education is closely tied to a local Māori community or *iwi*. This supports Māori as a living culture. There is a high expectation that *kura* graduates will have strong connections to their identity, language and culture and be successful in the Māori world, wider New Zealand and internationally.

There are currently 107 *kura*, out of a total of 2 529 New Zealand schools, although a number of predominantly English medium schools also offer Māori immersion, and bilingual classes, or the Māori language as a subject and it is embedded within the national curriculum for all students.

Māori medium schools are funded on the same basis as other public schools and face the same standards and accountability requirements as other schools. This includes the availability of additional per student funding which is higher for those participating in higher immersion levels. Students are expected to reach equivalent outcomes in terms of their curriculum levels and competencies, including literacy and numeracy. In Māori medium, there is an additional emphasis on being culturally competent members of *Te Ao Māori* (the Māori world) and highly proficient in the Māori language. Schools are required to report each year to parents on the progress their children are making in key learning areas and to provide achievement data to the Ministry of Education. The latter is made publicly available on an annual basis. Achievement data confirms that learners who attend *kōhanga reo* and *kura* (through to the end of Year 13) environments experience better outcomes in schooling and achieve consistently better school leaving qualifications than their peers in English medium schools.

Additionally, there is a strong correlation between Māori medium education participation and the proportion of Māori language speakers regionally.

Source: New Zealand Ministry of Education (2017), About Māori-medium education, https://education.govt.nz/ministry-of-education/specific-initiatives/nga-whanaketanga-rumaki-maori/about-maori-medium-education/.

In Australia, the Indigenous Language Perspectives team builds the capacity of teachers, schools, communities and regions across Queensland through professional development to support the various language learning needs of Aboriginal and Torres Strait Islander students, with their diverse and complex linguistic backgrounds. The team supports the implementation of the Australian Curriculum Framework for Aboriginal Languages and Torres Strait Islander Languages and raises awareness of community languages currently used by Aboriginal and Torres Strait Islander students and their families/communities. There is also a focus on EAL/D, offering coaching support for teachers and schools working with Indigenous EAL/D learners to build their understanding of language and teaching and particularly to lay the foundations to teach reading effectively. Queensland also led the development of the National Capability Framework for Teaching Aboriginal and Torres Strait Islander EAL/D learners. The Capability Framework aligns with and supports the implementation of the Australian Professional Standards for Teachers.

Beginning in 2016, under the heading of Acculturation of the Curriculum, New Brunswick is seeking to enhance the appropriateness of the curriculum for First Nation students, through an appreciation and understanding of First Nations history, language and culture. Development of culturally appropriate modules will be directly embedded in the existing curricular outcomes at each grade level. In some cases, new outcomes will need to be developed. This initiative has begun at Grade 9 level, and will continue into the middle and elementary levels. The high school Native Studies curriculum is currently being revised to address First Nation issues and the Truth and Reconciliation Commission's 94 Calls to Action.

Indigenous Perspectives - Curriculum and Pedagogy (IPCP) aims to empower teachers with knowledge and understanding of Australia's Aboriginal and Torres Strait peoples and the confidence to deliver lessons where embedding occurs. IPCP organises workshops and aims to develop greater understanding of Indigenous perspectives at a whole-school level. It supports the Australian Curriculum together with the complementary Aboriginal and Torres Strait Islander History and Cultures programme.

Insights on culture and language from the study visits

We repeatedly heard about the importance of language learning, Indigenous knowledge and the role of rituals and practices, as well as the need for culturally appropriate materials and programmes. There was also an acute awareness of the difficulties of recruiting adequate staff and trained Indigenous teachers. Indeed, this might be an area for further policy development in many systems, in terms of training successful Indigenous students to move into teaching positions as role models and as a means of helping to break down them-and-us attitudes. We also heard a lot about and saw examples of land-based programmes. At first sight, these might seem inappropriate for an increasingly urban, globalised world. Yet, as we pointed out in the opening chapter, the focus on the environment and sustainability, and the impetus to build connections between students, their communities and their physical environment have a very contemporary resonance. This applies to all students, Indigenous and non-Indigenous alike.

At the Three Nations Education Group Inc. in New Brunswick, we heard success defined as when students acquire both the Western and the Indigenous perspective. We also heard it described as when students know where they come from, acquire a sense of belonging, learn about culture and learn with an open heart. Students find it a barrier to learning, they said, if teachers do not know about First Nations culture and where their Indigenous students come from. They acknowledged some progress, but to date view it as a series of small steps.

A new framework for curriculum development on Treaty Education will impact teaching and learning in Nova Scotia. It was developed through co-operation between teachers and staff at Nova Scotia's Department of Education and Early Childhood Development as well as from *Mi'kmaw Kina'matnewey*, a First Nations-led Mi'kmaq Education Authority (in Nova Scotia). With the launch of the Minister's Action Plan on Education, aspects of treaty education have been implemented, and culturally responsive pedagogy has been introduced, for which specific dedicated professional development highlighting treaty education has been designed.

Yukon has developed a specific programme of First Nation Studies, which is intended to provide opportunities for students to explore human values and to measure their new knowledge against their own experiences. This is about the impact of the arrival of Europeans on Native societies and the social, economic and technological changes that occurred. It includes study of Canadian legislation, with emphasis on the reserve system and the making of treaties. To make the curriculum more relevant, there is an emphasis on land-based learning, and Yukon Education promotes the Rural Experiential Model, a week-long programme of intensive study that offers hands-on learning experiences to rural students by bringing them all together at one rural school. This covers a variety of programmes around land-based learning, although it may also raise tensions due to regulations concerning such things as safety. In addition to the First Hunt, First Fish programme, accredited culture camps with content set by the communities and taught using local resources, there is a wide variety of other programmes, including sensitivity training for all teachers, Yukon First Nations language programmes, bison hunts, bringing Elders to school and community feasts. At an elementary school we visited in Yukon, culture, languages and land-based learning are integral parts of the school. The school employs an education support worker who provides cultural activities for the children as well as a club for boys, and a community liaison co-ordinator, who is responsible for supporting positive relationships between the school and community.

At a school in the Northwest Territories, we heard that language education often involves collaborative teaching, partnering a trained teacher with another teacher and an Elder or other community member. Elders tend not to have pedagogic expertise, while trained teachers often do not speak the language. This can lead to fruitful collaboration in which, as we observed, the teachers lead a land-based exercise, and the Elder addresses specific knowledge and language, while classroom teachers are responsible for behaviour and particular students' needs.

One school we visited in a rural community in Alberta had been on the point of closing due to shrinking numbers of students. The non-Indigenous parents were keen to keep the school open, and through the principal building trust with local Indigenous communities, Indigenous students were enrolled by their parents and the school was able to remain open. This led to the introduction of Cree language teaching, ceremonies, the employment of an Indigenous support worker and teachers, as well as cultural activities in the school curriculum. The school offers a breakfast club for all students and introduced a flex period (involving different interventions), and there is an Indigenous community liaison officer. However, they have run into opposition from certain non-Indigenous parents, which the school leadership is resisting.

Addressing lack of trust and isolation

"It felt bizarre at the beginning that the community would not trust me because I am a teacher. In other contexts, that would be the other way around." (Teacher, Northwest Territories)

Community engagement requires relationships built on trust and integrity, sustained relationships between groups working towards shared goals. It will often mean that schools play a larger role as community hubs than they might in other systems or settings, using outreach and providing community services (Dreise and Thomson, 2014). This is an area in which a constant turnover of staff and leadership presents a real problem, as it compromises the building of sustained relationships.

In Nova Scotia, schools are trying to raise awareness with parents about self-identification (which is in place for all students), building trust so that people feel safe to self-identify. It is important that families know how and why these data are being collected. Data on the location of Indigenous students help school boards to inform the best placement of Indigenous student support workers in schools. Schools use the data to provide helpful information, such as potential scholarship opportunities for students. The province also uses the data to examine and monitor how students are doing on provincial assessments.

School Councils can be an important means to build connections between Indigenous parents and communities and schools. School Councils in Yukon have a larger responsibility than in many other parts of Canada. For example, they are involved in hiring the school principal and setting discipline and behaviour policies. Many First Nation governments employ a community support worker to liaise between schools and families. In First Nation communities, seats are guaranteed for an appointee of the Chief of the community. Most School Councils would define success, we heard, as making it possible for students in the community to go on from the school to the next level with confidence, and competence, including in finding work.

A mother who spoke to us at an elementary school in Alberta has several children at the school. She was happy to say that her children received the support they needed at the school and could learn in a safe and culturally-attuned environment. For her, success is when her children get the skills at school for lifelong learning, and she highlighted the importance of a strong community-school relationship. She is part of a large and active School Council. A key element of their activity is a weekly dinner, organised by the school for families. Another is the parents' numeracy programme, also organised by the school. These activities attract more parents to engage and to connect to other parents who are not yet involved in the school.

One of the main challenges raised in a meeting we attended in Yukon focused on the remoteness of schools and the related challenges, such as recruitment, community factors and social issues. Most teachers are from urban settings and may have difficulty adapting to a very remote setting. As a result, some may leave after only a short amount of time. Another major challenge of their remote location is ensuring the transition of students from remote rural communities to urban schools. Many such students face difficulties in making the transition to an urban school, and there is also is a concern about loss of the traditional life style in that process.

We visited a Yukon high school at which about 35 students come from rural communities to Whitehorse and live in a student residence as they finish their secondary education. Some are below the academic grade level of the other students when they arrive at the school, which makes the transition even more difficult. This is in addition to the cultural adaptation for students who are far away from their families and communities, and for some families it is an uneasy reminder of the residential school system. If they are from a remote community, once installed in Whitehorse, they may have few opportunities to go home other than at defined breaks during the school year. There is communal life in the residence, and there are support workers to help. But some students still struggle to cope with the town and institutional life and eventually drop out. In this context, we heard about the Friendship Centre in Whitehorse as a point of contact for First Nation students and their families. The Friendship Centre offers career advice, work placements, first aid, clothing, and support for students through job and counselling services.

Staff at a school in Whitehorse feel that the Be the Change programme has changed the school profoundly. Teachers, students and staff have been more caring since its introduction, and the programme has reinforced an open and flexible climate with increased cohesion in the school. It is targeted at Grade 8 students, but engages the whole school and the community. It is an experimental and self-reflective way to explore racism, gender and other issues, in line with First Nations restorative practices. The programme starts with a whole day of activities that challenge everybody to do things differently.

Addressing isolation, examples from Queensland

Students who graduate from remote primary schools on Cape York, the Northern Peninsula Area and the Torres Strait often have to leave their home communities to attend boarding secondary school placements. Transition Support Services (TSS) helps students and their families to address transition challenges and develop opportunities to enable students to stay in school. TSS employs Transition Support Teachers and Officers to work with students at their boarding schools, as well as with staff and families. If young people become disconnected and return to their home communities, TSS works in collaboration with many remote service providers to assist young people and their families to develop and enact a re-engagement action plan. The Supporting Students Initiative in Queensland is about creating additional guidance counsellors in schools (45 full-time-equivalent positions) to address issues of isolation and help inform pathways.

The Remote Area Incentive Scheme addresses material and other aspects of the well-being of teachers in rural and remote schools by opening access to financial benefits, more career opportunities and assistance to move. There are 35 Aboriginal and Torres Strait Islander Early Years Services (Remote Services) located in remote areas of Queensland. They offer culturally appropriate services that meet local community needs for children (from birth to age 8) and their families who identify as Aboriginal and/or Torres Strait Islander. These services take the form of financial support or are integrated hubs, long day-care centres, care services outside school hours, children's activity centres, limited-hours care services, vacation or holiday care programmes, family support programmes and playgroups.

More widely applicable in Australia, the Remote Indigenous Professional Development project promotes understanding and use of the Early Years Learning Framework (EYLF) for Aboriginal and Torres Strait Islander early-childhood educators in remote areas of Queensland, the Northern Territory and South Australia. The project aims to meet the learning needs of entry-level educators as they build on their understanding and implementation of the EYLF through Aboriginal and Torres Strait Islander ways of doing and learning.

Teachers

Recruitment and retention of teachers to take on the wide range of new responsibilities described in this section are clearly major issues. Finding teachers from Indigenous communities who are role models and can speak their Indigenous language is a significant challenge. In Nova Scotia, for instance, we heard about the extremely limited numbers of Mi'kmaq teachers in the public school system. There is a struggle for school environments to be both receptive and responsive to their Indigenous students' needs, especially in places where there may be only one Indigenous teacher on staff. In Manitoba, we heard that teachers need confidence to teach Indigenous topics, including on the legacy of residential schools, while knowing what is most appropriate to leave to Elders. In answer to a question about the achievement gap in New Brunswick, we heard that "... there is more a teaching gap than an achievement gap; sometimes the teachers do not see the students in the school, they do not see it as their responsibility, and they need to bridge the cultural gaps."

Mentoring should be one element of appropriate strategies. The Indigenous Mentoring Programme in Queensland aims to strengthen the leadership skills of Aboriginal and Torres Strait Islander educators to support children's learning, development and cultural well-being. The six-month mentoring programme is facilitated by Aboriginal and Torres Strait Islander pedagogical leaders in early childhood education.

With a wide definition of the role of the school comes a correspondingly wide definition of the responsibilities of teachers. In the Northwest Territories, it was acknowledged that building relationships with communities takes time and leads to a heavy workload for the teachers. There are many unqualified teachers in schools, as it is difficult to hire qualified teachers. One indication of the recognition of the important role of teachers in this context is Alberta's inclusion of additional questions in the 2018 OECD Teaching and Learning International Survey pertaining to teachers' and school leaders' understanding of issues related to Indigenous cultures, history and working with Indigenous students, as well as on relevant professional development.

In our view, addressing teachers and school leaders and clarifying recruitment practices and roles of community support staff are very high priorities in the quest to improve education for Indigenous populations.

Psychological and physical health

Psychological health and physical health are central dimensions of well-being. The holistic approach of Indigenous peoples stresses how much these contribute to the overall well-being of children, as well as everyone else, in addition to factors such as material advantage and disadvantage. The trauma suffered by Indigenous peoples, including through the residential school system, is still acutely felt by many. Indeed, we were told that the symptoms of trauma may be increasing rather than diminishing with the passage of time, exacerbated through intergenerational relationships.

Measures of these dimensions of well-being are put into context by the Canadian national picture, as surveyed through the Health Behaviour in School-Aged Children Survey. Against this bigger picture, specific surveys of particular provinces and territories, and comparing Indigenous and non-Indigenous young people, can be better understood (Freeman, King and Pickett, 2016).

Psychological, mental and emotional well-being

There are no Canada-wide data pertaining specifically to Indigenous young people. Among all young people, relatively low levels (around 50%) report high life satisfaction, and that declines as students advance in age and move to higher grades through their school life. This is as might be expected, but life satisfaction also seems to be declining over time. There are also particular problems of psychological well-being for girls.

The percentage of students reporting emotional concerns increased across grade levels. Consistently, a larger percentage of girls than boys reported internalizing characteristics on question items related to sadness or hopelessness, feeling lonely, and feeling nervous. In addition, a greater percentage of girls than boys indicated the presence of psychosomatic symptoms (headaches, stomach aches, feeling irritable or bad tempered) at least once a week during the past six months.

[...]

In terms of prosocial behaviours, a higher proportion of girls than boys across grade levels reported prosocial actions or behaviours. Across survey administration years, the percentage of students rating high life satisfaction varied from just above to just below half of all students. There was a steady decrease in the percentage of students affirming a high level of life satisfaction, with lower proportions noted for girls compared to boys for each year of the survey administration (with the exception of 2006). A notable trend emerging from the analysis of data was the association between strong social support, particularly family support, and high life satisfaction. This finding underscores the critical role that positive relationships and strong social networks play in contributing to and enhancing students' psychological well-being. (Morrison and Peterson, 2016, pp.127-128)

Specific findings in provinces and territories

As previously mentioned, New Brunswick conducts a specific survey of student wellness, in which it can distinguish between Indigenous and non-Indigenous students. Low numbers of students report high mental fitness, and the numbers are lower still for the Indigenous students (Table 4.2).

Table 4.2. New Brunswick Student Wellness Survey, results on mental fitness, Grades 6-12, 2012/13

Survey topic	Indigenous students (%)	Non-Indigenous students (%)	Gap between Indigenous and non-Indigenous students (%)
High level of mental fitness	16	26	-10
Medium level of mental fitness	53	53	0
Low level of mental fitness	31	21	10

Source: New Brunswick Health Council (2013), www.nbhc.ca/surveys/nbsws#.WSMBE2996Uk.

In the recent Stakeholder Satisfaction with Education in Alberta surveys, the questions asked, among other things, how well schools are contributing to students' development of emotional well-being (Alberta Education, 2016). Among high school students, whether Indigenous or not, the levels of those satisfied have been falling in the years from 2012 to 2016. Overall, the differences between Indigenous and non-Indigenous respondents are small. Parents tend to be less convinced than students that schools are contributing to emotional well-being, with Indigenous parents least convinced, although in 2016 the gap between Indigenous parents of K-12 students and all parents of K-12 Alberta students had been reversed.

Youth in the Northwest Territories reported poorer results in most mental health indicators than students in the rest of Canada. Female students reported a higher level of emotional problems than both males in the Northwest Territories and females in the rest of Canada. Both male and female students reported lower levels of prosocial behaviour and life satisfaction than the national average. As within Canada as a whole, there are particular problems reported for girls in the Northwest Territories.

Physical well-being and health

For Canada as a whole, there are a number of areas of concern about health-related activities (Janssen, 2016; Freeman, 2016; Saewyc, 2016). Many young people do not eat well. Only one in ten Canadian youths adhere to the Canadian non-sedentary behaviour guidelines, and the proportion of students meeting guidelines for physical activity and non-sedentary behaviour decreases considerably between Grade 6 and Grade 10. By Grade 9, approximately six in ten boys and seven in ten girls report that they go to school tired, and around a third of boys and a quarter of the girls are overweight or obese (self-reported height and weight). But there are also more encouraging findings. Diets appear to have improved over time, and rates of daily smoking continue to be low for Canadian students. Beer drinking continues to decline, and cannabis consumption is at the lowest level reported by students over the past 20 years.

Of the provincial data that distinguishes Indigenous and non-Indigenous students, New Brunswick Wellness Survey information from 2012/13 suggests problematic levels of physical fitness for both student populations, although self-reporting on such things as having a healthy weight may not be especially reliable. Around four in ten students said that they were not physically active in the week prior to the survey, and only a third of Indigenous students reported regularly taking part in competitive team sports (Table 4.3).

Table 4.3. New Brunswick Student Wellness Survey, results on physical fitness, Grades 6-12, 2012/13

Survey Topic	Indigenous students (%)	Non-Indigenous students (%)	Gap between Indigenous and non-Indigenous students (%)
Respondent was not physically active in the week prior to the survey	37	40	-3
Respondent has a healthy weight	56	66	-10
Respondent participates in competitive school sports teams	34	40	-6
Respondent is physically active at least one hour daily	63	60	3

Source: New Brunswick Health Council (2013), www.nbhc.ca/surveys/nbsws#.WSMBE2996Uk.

The HBSC study focusing specifically on the Northwest Territories (Freeman et al., 2012), was based on the starting point that: "In the Northwest Territories (NWT), schools play a much more central role in health promotion than in many other parts of Canada. Schools are a significant focal point of every NWT community, often serving in capacities that are additional to their mandate." Youth in the Northwest Territories reported poorer results in most mental health indicators than students in the rest of Canada. Female students in the Northwest Territories reported higher levels of emotional problem than both males in the Northwest Territories and females in the rest of Canada. Both male and female students reported lower levels of prosocial behaviour and life satisfaction than the national average. Issues related to obesity and low physical activity have been identified as requiring special attention, as have relationships with others.

Dreise and Thomson (2014) refer to "emerging models such as the Connected Communities strategy in New South Wales [that] are repositioning schools to become hubs which facilitate access to other support services for Indigenous children and people such as health, employment and community services (p.4)". Such an example in the Northwest Territories is the partnership represented by the Healthy Choices Framework. This is an interdepartmental committee which helps co-ordinate health promotion. However, the need for partnerships extends well beyond government departments, ideally including schools, school boards, community organisations, Indigenous governments, non-governmental organisations and other stakeholders. Schools Plus in Nova Scotia is a collaborative interagency approach supporting children and their families, with the school as the centre of service delivery. There is a data/information-sharing agreement with more than 200 schools and a transition task force to help students, through training programmes and individual career plans.

Sometimes, the partnership works at the very local level. In one school we visited in the Northwest Territories, when it becomes known that a woman is pregnant, a meeting is arranged to provide information about healthy eating, screening services, etc., and there is follow-up with her once the child is born. This includes strong encouragement to enrol the child in preschool. The school organises parenting workshops throughout the year on topics such as healthy eating. A learning centre in the Yukon integrates services such as housing, health and social services with the early learning centre, and it offers a variety of language and cultural activities for the very young, while strongly involving parents. In another Yukon school we visited, and for students who become parents early in their lives, there is a teen parent centre in which student mothers receive prenatal and postnatal nutrition care, health screenings, parenting help, day care and help to find employment and to acquire a driver's licence. Similarly, families living in Yarmouth, Nova Scotia have access to the Parenting Journey Programme, part of Stronger Families Nova Scotia, which aims to strengthen child welfare and early intervention. The goal is to work more closely with community partners to meet the diverse needs of families in need of support. The programme is being expanded to 15 more communities and organisations throughout the province.

There are concerns about mental well-being, not only for students, but for teachers as well. Several teachers we met discussed the strain teachers face in isolated settings and an increasing focus on the mental and physical health of teachers. One approach being developed is the Mindfulness programme, which is accessible online to all teachers. In another school district, a community of practice has been created among teachers to tackle isolation. The teachers meet twice a year in person and twice a month online, and many more teachers than expected participated in this programme. Sometimes two or three teachers go together to a remote area to teach as a group, so they will be less alone in the communities, but often they all leave at the same time, which creates problems for continuity.

One foundation for developing health literacy partnerships is to share a common base through guides and easily accessible information. One such guide has been developed through the Winnipeg Health Region in Manitoba. Now in its fourth edition, The *Culture of Well-being: Guide to Mental Health Resources for First Nations, Metis and Inuit People in Winnipeg* was compiled by the Winnipeg Regional Health Authority's Indigenous Health programme, in collaboration with its Mental Health programme.

Queensland has ten Children and Family Centres that integrate early childhood development, child and maternal health and family support services for children from birth to age 8 who are identified as Aboriginal and/or Torres Strait Islander and their families. The services and programmes are culturally appropriate and delivered from purpose-built facilities. The Be well Learn well programme in Queensland applies strategies that integrate education and health methods to support Aboriginal and Torres Strait Islander student developmental needs in remote schools. The project focuses on treating the underlying factors that affect education and learning outcomes. Allied health staff from a range of specialisms address behavioural and learning issues for Aboriginal and Torres Strait Islander students. The six schools receiving allied health care are located in remote geographic locations with limited specialist services. Another example is Solid Choices, Healthy Futures, a sexual health curriculum developed through an intergovernmental partnership between Queensland Health and the Department of Education and Training, to foster students' health literacy.

Queensland also has 25 sites in the Families as First Teachers (FaFT) programme, which has been running since 2005. These sites are located in and funded by state schools, health centres, local councils, and Child and Family Centres. They aim to: 1) build the capacity and leadership of local Aboriginal and Torres Strait Islander staff implementing FaFT; 2) strengthen Aboriginal and Torres Strait Islander ownership and build the capacity of parents/carers in early learning; 3) create resources for home use; 4) provide opportunities for parents to meet with and support one another; 5) address the transition from home to formal education settings; 6) embed culture and language in early learning; and 7) build children's early literacy and numeracy skills.

Hence, the most promising practices to promote healthy living and wellness emphasise integrated approaches that see health issues as an integral part of educational policy, regard education as an integral aspect of wider well-being, develop schools as hubs of different social services and interactions, and address families as well as schools.

Notes

1. For further information on the treaty, see: www.teara.govt.nz/en/treaty-of-waitangi.

2. Solid partners Solid futures: A partnership approach for excellence in Aboriginal and Torres Strait Islander early childhood, education, training and employment from 2013 to 2016: http://msctece.weebly.com/uploads/2/0/7/1/20719370/atsi-solid-partners-solid-futures.pdf.

3. For further information, see: http://kep.org.nz/assets/resources/site/Voices7-12.The-Kia-Eke-Panuku-Team.pdf.

4. For further information, see: https://educationcouncil.org.nz/content/graduating-teacher-standards.

5. For further information, see: https://educationcouncil.org.nz/sites/default/files/Tataiako.pdf.

6. For further information, see: https://education.alberta.ca/provincial-satisfaction-surveys/about-the-surveys/everyone/provincial-satisfaction-surveys-faq/.

References

Aber, J.L. et al. (1997), "The Effects of Poverty on Child Health and Development", *Annual Review of Public Health,* Vol. 18/1, pp. 463-483, http://dx.doi.org/10.1146/annurev.publhealth.18.1.463.

Alberta Education (2016), *Stakeholder Satisfaction with Education in Alberta Surveys: Summary Report*, Alberta Education, Edmonton, https://education.alberta.ca/media/3401931/alberta-education-survey-summary-report-2016.pdf.

Borgonovi, F. and J. Pál (2016), "A Framework for the Analysis of Student Well-being in the PISA 2015 Study: Being 15 in 2015", *OECD Education Working Papers*, No. 140, OECD Publishing, Paris, http://dx.doi.org/10.1787/5jlpszwghvvb-en.

Case, A., A. Fertig and C. Paxson (2005), "The lasting impact of childhood health and circumstance", *Journal of Health Economics*, 24 (2005), pp. 365-389, www.princeton.edu/~accase/downloads/The_Lasting_Impact_of_Childhood_Health_and_Circumstance.pdf.

Doyle, L. and R. Hill (2008*), Our Children, Our Future: Achieving Improved Primary and Secondary Education Outcomes for Indigenous Students: An overview of investment opportunities and approaches*, Social Ventures Australia, Sydney, http://socialventures.com.au/assets/Our_Children_Our_Future.pdf.

Dreise, T. and W. Perrett (forthcoming), "Promising Practices in Closing The Gap in Indigenous Education: A Literature Review Report for the OECD", OECD Publishing, Paris.

Dreise, T. and S. Thomson (2014), "Unfinished business: PISA shows Indigenous youth are being left behind", *ACER Occasional Essays*, ACER, Melbourne, February, http://research.acer.edu.au/indigenous_education/37.

Fraillon, J. (2004), "Measuring Student Well-Being in the Context of Australian Schooling: Discussion Paper", Commissioned by the South Australian Department of Education and Children's Services, Ministerial Council on Education, Employment, Training and Youth Affairs, www.curriculum.edu.au/verve/_resources/Measuring_Student_Well-Being_in_the_Context_of_Australian_Schooling.pdf.

Freeman, J. (2016), "Healthy Eating", in J. Freeman, M. King and W. Pickett (eds.), *Health Behaviour in School-Aged Children (HBSC) in Canada: Focus on Relationships*, pp. 83-94, Public Health Agency of Canada, Ottawa, http://healthycanadians.gc.ca/publications/science-research-sciences-recherches/health-behaviour-children-canada-2015-comportements-sante-jeunes/index-eng.php#c8.

Freeman, J. et al. (2012), *Health and Health-Related Behaviours Among Young People in the Northwest Territories*, Northwest Territories Legislative Assembly, Yellowknife, www.assembly.gov.nt.ca/sites/default/files/12-11-06td105-173.pdf.

Freeman, J., M. King and W. Pickett (eds.) (2016), *Health Behaviour in School-Aged Children (HBSC) in Canada: Focus on Relationships*, Public Health Agency of Canada, Ottawa, http://healthycanadians.gc.ca/publications/science-research-sciences-recherches/health-behaviour-children-canada-2015-comportements-sante-jeunes/alt/health-behaviour-children-canada-2015-comportements-sant%C3%A9-jeunes-eng.pdf.

Gariépy, G. et al. (2016), "Community", in J. Freeman, M. King and W. Pickett (eds.), *Health Behaviour in School-Aged Children (HBSC) in Canada: Focus on Relationships*, pp. 55-64, Public Health Agency of Canada, Ottawa, http://healthy canadians.gc.ca/publications/science-research-sciences-recherches/health-behaviour-children-canada-2015-comportements-sante-jeunes/alt/health-behaviour-children-canada-2015-comportements-sant%C3%A9-jeunes-eng.pdf.

Haswell, M. et al. (2013), *The Social and Emotional Wellbeing of Indigenous Youth: Reviewing and Extending the Evidence and Examining its Implications for Policy and Practice*, Muru Marri, School of Public Health and Community Medicine, University of New South Wales, Sydney, https://sphcm.med.unsw.edu.au/sites/default/files/sphcm/Centres_and_Units/IYSEWB_ResearchReport_MM.pdf.

Janssen, I. (2016), "Physical Activity and Sedentary Behaviour", in J. Freeman, M. King and W. Pickett (eds.), *Health Behaviour in School-Aged Children (HBSC) in Canada: Focus on Relationships*, pp. 65-74, Public Health Agency of Canada, Ottawa, http://healthycanadians.gc.ca/publications/science-research-sciences-recherches/health-behaviour-children-canada-2015-comportements-sante-jeunes/alt/health-behaviour-children-canada-2015-comportements-sant%C3%A9-jeunes-eng.pdf.

Manitoba Education and Advanced Learning (2014), *Manitoba Provincial Report: Tell Them from Me: Bullying and School Safety*, Manitoba Education and Advanced Learning, Winnipeg, www.edu.gov.mb.ca/k12/safe_schools/ttfm/full_doc.pdf.

Morrison, B. and P. Peterson (2016), "Mental Health", in J. Freeman, M. King and W. Pickett (eds.), *Health Behaviour in School-aged Children (HBSC) in Canada: Focus on Relationships*, pp. 55-64, Public Health Agency of Canada, Ottawa, http://healthycanadians.gc.ca/publications/science-research-sciences-recherches/health-behaviour-children-canada-2015-comportements-sante-jeunes/alt/health-behaviour-children-canada-2015-comportements-sant%C3%A9-jeunes-eng.pdf.

Mulford, B. (2011), "Teacher and school leader quality and sustainability", Resource sheet no. 5, Closing the Gap Clearinghouse, Australian Government, Australian Institute of Health and Welfare and Australian Institute of Family Studies, www.aihw.gov.au/uploadedFiles/ClosingTheGap/Content/Publications/2011/ctgc-rs05.pdf.

New Brunswick Health Council (2013), New Brunswick Student Wellness Survey, New Brunswick Health Council, Moncton, www.nbhc.ca/surveys/nbsws.

New Zealand Ministry of Education (2017), About Māori-medium education, https://education.govt.nz/ministry-of-education/specific-initiatives/nga-whanaketanga-rumaki-maori/about-maori-medium-education/.

Nguyen, O.K. and S. Cairney (2013), "Literature review of the interplay between education, employment, health and wellbeing for Aboriginal and Torres Strait Islander people in remote areas: Working towards an Aboriginal and Torres Strait Islander wellbeing framework" ,CRC-REP Working Paper CW013, Ninti One Limited, Alice Springs, https://nintione.com.au/resource/CW013_InterplayLiteratureReview_TowardsWellbeingFramework.pdf.

OECD (2013), *PISA 2012 Results: Excellence through Equity (Volume II): Giving Every Student the Chance to Succeed*, OECD Publishing, Paris, http://dx.doi.org/10.1787/9789264201132-en.

OECD (2011), *How's Life?: Measuring Well-being*, OECD Publishing, Paris. http://dx.doi.org/10.1787/9789264121164-en.

Pollard, E. and P. Lee (2003), "Child Well-being: A Systematic Review of the Literature", *Social Indicators Research*, Vol. 61, pp. 59-78.

Rath, T., J. Harter and J. K. Harter (2010), *Wellbeing: The Five Essential Elements*, Gallup Press, New York, NY.

Ritchie, S.D. et al. (2014), "Promoting resilience and wellbeing through an outdoor intervention designed for Aboriginal adolescents", *The International Electronic Journal of Rural and Remote Health Research, Education 14:2523, Practice and Policy*, www.rrh.org.au/publishedarticles/article_print_2523.pdf.

Saewyc, E. (2016), "Substance Use", in J. Freeman, M. King and W. Pickett (eds.), *Health Behaviour in School-Aged Children (HBSC) in Canada: Focus on Relationships*, pp. 145-160, Public Health Agency of Canada, Ottawa, http://healthycanadians.gc.ca/publications/science-research-sciences-recherches/health-behaviour-children-canada-2015-comportements-sante-jeunes/alt/health-behaviour-children-canada-2015-comportements-sant%C3%A9-jeunes-eng.pdf.

Statham, J. and E. Chase (2010), *Childhood Wellbeing: A brief overview*, Childhood Wellbeing Research Centre, Briefing Paper 1, London, www.cwrc.ac.uk/documents/CWRC_Briefing_paper.pdf.

Chapter 5

Increasing the participation of Indigenous students in education

Participation in education reflects students' access to education and their opportunities to learn. Although the overall level of participation is high across the jurisdictions in the study, Indigenous students have lower levels of participation than non-Indigenous students. Limited access to opportunities can have a significant impact on a student's later outcomes. This chapter outlines the importance of participation in education for positive student development, from the early years to the senior years. It also covers progress in monitoring participation across the jurisdictions and identifies patterns of participation according to many factors, including gender, socio-economic status and geographic location. The study has identified a number of promising policies and practices to support Indigenous students' participation in education.

Students' participation in education reflects their access to education and opportunities to learn. In most education systems, there are some students who are not continuously enrolled in either early childhood education and care (ECEC) or school, or who drop out of school at some point. This can be related to many factors, including whether schools are inclusive and relevant to all students. But students have a right to education and a right to expect that actions will be taken to resolve the issues that have kept them out of the system. To take such actions, education systems must be able to monitor student participation at the individual level and the aggregate level.

This chapter identifies where Indigenous student participation rates have improved, based on evidence provided by the participating jurisdictions. In this context, in Canada participation refers to the enrolment rate, the number of students (Indigenous and non-Indigenous) enrolled in provincial/territorial schools as a proportion of the number of students (Indigenous and non-Indigenous) who live in the province or territory, minus those students enrolled in on-reserve schools.[1]

The evidence provided shows significant gaps in the participation rates of Indigenous and non-Indigenous students across all age groups in the Canadian provinces and territories participating in this study. These gaps do not appear to be closing.

New Zealand and Queensland also have differences in the participation rates of Indigenous and non-Indigenous students, although these are smaller than experienced in the Canadian provinces and territories in this study. Between 2005 and 2015, the participation rates of Indigenous students in New Zealand increased, although in terms of overall years of basic education non-Indigenous students in New Zealand participate, on average, for one additional year.

In Canadian provinces and territories, as well as in New Zealand and Queensland, there are a range of policies and practices that support improvements in student participation rates.[2] In Canada, the most promising efforts appear to be led by individual education and community leaders. While these initiatives have a positive impact on the Indigenous students in these communities, these pockets of excellence do not translate into sustained, system-wide improvements. In both New Zealand and Australia, improvements have been led both at the system level and by individual communities and schools. Where these efforts are aligned and mutually reinforcing, the impact is more positive than reliance solely on system-wide efforts or solely on interventions by individual communities or schools.

The chapter covers the importance of participation in education for positive student outcomes, progress in monitoring participation across the participating jurisdictions, participation patterns, and policies and practices to improve participation in education.

Why participation matters

Education systems around the world have pursued different strategies to get children to school, from banning child labour and early marriage to offering compulsory free schooling, with positive results overall (Barro and Lee, 2013). The rationale behind compulsory education is that learning occurs primarily, (although not exclusively) in school, and that higher enrolment and attainment rates benefit both individuals and society as a whole (Lleras-Muney, 2002; Oreopoulos, 2006).

Participation in education is a necessary but not sufficient condition for positive student outcomes, as set out in the analytic framework for this study. In addition to participation in education, student well-being and engagement are also critical to achieve positive student outcomes. This section addresses three key aspects relating to participation: 1) ensuring sufficient years of participation to achieve educational success; 2) the positive and enduring impact of a strong, early start; and 3) the importance of retention in the senior schooling years.

Ensuring sufficient years of participation to achieve educational success

As demonstrated through the OECD Programme for International Student Assessment (PISA), education systems with poorer student performance tend to provide fewer overall years of basic education[3] than the average for OECD countries. Student participation in such countries is generally characterised by a late start and an early finish, resulting in low participation rates in the early and senior years of schooling. While early entry to education, such as through ECEC, particularly supports better relative PISA results, an early finish in school reduces the likely acquisition of school-based qualifications and access to higher education.

Figure 5.1. Mathematics performance and number of years of basic education

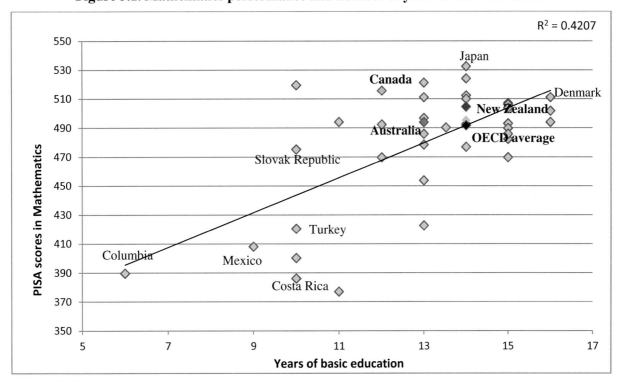

Sources: OECD (2016a), PISA 2015 Database, www.oecd.org/pisa/data/2015database/; OECD (2016b), *Education at a Glance 2016: OECD Indicators*, http://dx.doi.org/10.1787/eag-2016-en.

Many other factors affect overall student performance, including out-of-school factors (such as students' background) and in-school factors (such as the quality of teaching). However, as noted previously, students who do not receive sufficient years of basic education do not have sufficient opportunities for learning to ensure their success (Figure 5.1). This is particularly important for students from disadvantaged backgrounds, for whom school may be their main means to develop skills.

Canadian students, on average, experience fewer years of basic education than the average for OECD countries (Figure 5.2).

Figure 5.2. Number of years of basic education in OECD countries, 2014

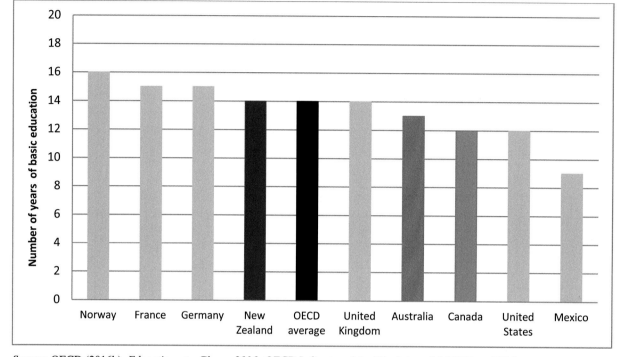

Source: OECD (2016b), *Education at a Glance 2016: OECD Indicators*, http://dx.doi.org/10.1787/eag-2016-en.

As noted above, the impact of the number of years of education also depends on a range of other factors, such as children's home background and the quality of teaching. Reaching close to the OECD average number of years of education appears to provide a protective factor for students in improving the likelihood of academic success. This largely arises because to reach the OECD average of 14 years, students need to enter the education system at age 3 or 4 and remain in it until age 17 or 18.

The positive and enduring impact of a strong early start

Evidence on the positive impacts of early skill development on a broad range of positive outcomes during adolescence and adulthood is consistent and compelling (Bartik, 2014; Duncan and Soujourner, 2013; Duncan and Magnuson, 2013). Early skill development starts primarily in the home, building on early attachment, with activities between children and their parents and/or caregivers being the main determinant of early learning.

As demonstrated in the Effective Pre-Primary Education (EPPE) longitudinal study in the United Kingdom (Sylva et al., 2004), activities such as talking and reading with infants, singing songs and reciting nursery rhymes, and counting and other games have more impact on child development than any other factor, including socio-economic status. The EPPE study concluded that what parents do is much more important for children's development than who they are, in terms of socio-economic status, education levels, and racial and linguistic backgrounds.

Thus, early childhood education and care and other interventions that help families to understand and support the development of their young children can provide huge benefits. When children's early development has not progressed well in the initial years, ECEC can be effective in helping children to get back on track in their development, especially in key areas such as language. In addition, ECEC can assist children to develop other key skills such as self-regulation, empathy, trust in others, prosocial skills, gross and fine motor skills and early numeracy (OECD, forthcoming).

For children from disadvantaged backgrounds, the provision of high-quality ECEC can be hugely positive and enduring. A meta-analysis of longitudinal studies of disadvantaged children in targeted ECEC programmes found significant positive impacts on outcomes for these children throughout schooling and into adulthood. The effects are positive in terms of later education achievement, employment and earnings, and health and social outcomes. The effects are significant, and they persist into middle age, (i.e. at age 50) (Bartik, 2014).

The positive effects of prior participation in ECEC are also seen in scores for nearly all countries that participate in PISA, including Canada. According to 2015 PISA results, students who had attended pre-primary school for more than one year score higher than students who had attended for less time. Indeed, students who had attended between two and three years of pre-primary school score 35 points higher than students who did not attend and 50 score points higher than students who had attended less than one year, on average (Figure 5.3).

Figure 5.3. ECEC attendance and PISA scores, 2015

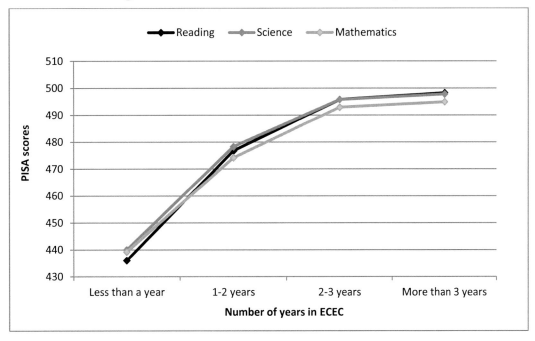

Source: OECD (2016a), PISA 2015 Database, www.oecd.org/pisa/data/2015database/.

ECEC participation rates have been increasing across OECD countries for more than a decade. On average, across OECD countries with 2005 and 2014 data, enrolments of 3-year-olds in pre-primary education rose from 54% in 2005 to 69% in 2014, and enrolments of 4-year-olds rose from 73% in 2005 to 85% in 2014. The enrolment rate of

4-year-olds in pre-primary education increased by 32 percentage points in Australia, between 2005 and 2014, from 53% to 85%. In New Zealand, 92% of 4-year-olds participated in ECEC in 2014 (the 2005 enrolment rate of 4-year-olds is not available for New Zealand). Rates for Canada are not reported (OECD, 2016b).

While much of the growth in ECEC over the last two decades has coincided with increased labour market participation of women, there is increasing awareness among policy makers, education leaders and practitioners, and parents of the role that ECEC can play in enhancing children's well-being and cognitive and social-emotional development, including in mitigating social inequalities. Many of the inequalities found in education systems are already evident when children enter formal schooling and persist or increase as they progress through the school system.

As well as boosting overall performance in PISA, participation in ECEC also appears to provide students with a protective factor against low performance. Without any pre-primary education, students were more than twice as likely to be below the baseline proficiency in PISA than students who had completed more than one year of pre-primary education. (OECD, 2016a).

The importance of retention in senior schooling

In the past, upper secondary education was mainly designed to prepare an elite for university studies, but this part of schooling systems now plays a key role in ensuring that young people leave the education system with the basic qualifications and skills required for employability and successful functioning in society. The OECD's annual indicators on education and associated labour market outcomes suggest that completion of upper secondary education now marks the minimum threshold for successful labour market entry and continued employability. Furthermore, it is the stepping stone to opportunities in further education (OECD, 2015).

Students who drop out of the education system and leave school without an upper secondary qualification tend to face severe difficulties entering and remaining in the labour market. They face more precarious and lower-paid employment options, and their opportunities for further education and training are generally more limited than students who successfully complete their secondary education.

Graduating from upper secondary education has become increasingly important in all countries, as the skills needed in the labour market are becoming more knowledge-based, and workers are progressively required to adapt to the uncertainties of a rapidly changing global economy. However, while graduation rates give an indication of the extent to which education systems are succeeding in preparing students to meet the minimum requirements of the labour market, they do not capture the quality of education outcomes or wider benefits for students (OECD, 2016b).

Upper secondary schooling often represents a challenging change for students. It gives them the opportunity to choose the content of their studies to a significant extent, in tracks and courses reflecting their various interests and academic or professional goals. Many education systems divide students into separate types of education at the upper secondary level, with different qualifications at the end of the programmes and different expectations of transition to further education or work. In particular, students can generally choose between academic programmes that lead to tertiary education and vocational or technical programmes that provide training for particular jobs in the labour market (OECD, 2012).

Upper secondary schooling tends to last between two to five years in most OECD countries. While upper secondary education is not compulsory in most OECD countries, approximately 90% of OECD young people leaving lower secondary education enrol in it, and the remaining 10% leave the education system without relevant qualifications. However, between 10% and 30% of students starting upper secondary do not complete it. While some may recover through adult education and second-chance programmes, one of five young people have still not completed upper secondary or the equivalent by age 34 (OECD, 2012).

At senior levels of schooling, the motivation for participating in education changes. Participation is often less about the social, sporting and other opportunities provided at school, and more about whether students see that they are developing new skills and making progress in their educational pathway.

Among the main challenges the OECD has identified for upper secondary education is delivering relevant education that addresses varied students' needs and supporting effective transitions by preparing young adults for work or further education. The existence of different tracks in upper secondary education (academic, vocational and technical) can present a challenge to equity, but also an opportunity to complete secondary education, if the tracks are well designed (OECD, 2012).

Progress in monitoring participation

Developing and maintaining reliable data on the participation of particular groups of students can be challenging. Students and their families may be reluctant to self-identify as Indigenous, reflecting uncertainty about how such information might be used. Schools may be reluctant to ask for and relay such information to central authorities. The lack of central, ongoing recording systems means that children who are not in education cannot be identified, students and their families are asked to self-identify more than once, and students who change schools or move to another province or territory cannot be tracked to ensure they are enrolled in another school. Also, there is a lack of integration between the provincial/territorial systems for recording students attending their public and private schools and the federal system for recording students attending on-reserve schools.

Increased monitoring of enrolment numbers has occurred across jurisdictions. Only New Zealand and Queensland could provide data on the enrolment numbers for Indigenous students for 2005. For 2010, this increased to include Alberta, Manitoba and the Northwest Territories. For 2015, both Nova Scotia and Yukon were also able to provide data on enrolment numbers for Indigenous students. New Brunswick does record the numbers of Indigenous students enrolled in its schools, but only for those students who live on a reserve.

There is, however, an important distinction between enrolment numbers and enrolment rates. Enrolment rates are needed to monitor progress in ensuring that all children are accessing the education they are entitled to. This information is also needed to assess the overall impacts of policies and local efforts to increase participation rates. To accurately assess enrolment rates, jurisdictions need to know how many Indigenous students reside in the province or territory, the ages of these students and the number and ages of students attending on-reserve schools. This is the only way for jurisdictions to monitor and manage participation. New Zealand is the only jurisdiction in this study that is currently able to do this with confidence.

Overall participation patterns

In both New Zealand and Queensland, overall years of education of Indigenous students are lower than those of non-Indigenous students. In the Canadian jurisdictions in this study, the difference in years of education between Indigenous students and non-Indigenous students is even starker.

Figure 5.4 shows the number of years of basic education (ECEC and schooling) of Indigenous students compared to all students. Across the Canadian jurisdictions in this study that had data on Indigenous student enrolments, less than 90% of Indigenous students are enrolled at every grade level.[4] With such low participation rates, Indigenous students in Canada are clearly not receiving the same educational opportunities as other Canadian students. This is a fundamental issue that will require a whole-of-system response.

Figure 5.4. Number of years of ECEC and schooling for Indigenous students compared to all students, 2015

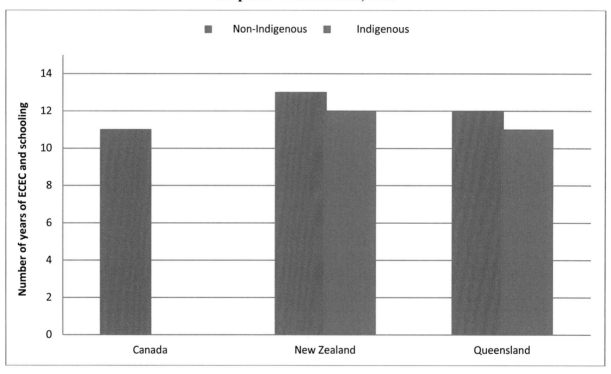

Note: Schooling refers to the number of years at which at least 90% of the population of students are enrolled. In the figure, Canadian data include only Alberta, Manitoba, Nova Scotia and Yukon. Since less than 90% of Indigenous students are enrolled at every grade level, the number of years of schooling is reported as 0.

Sources: Alberta Education, Manitoba Education, Nova Scotia Education, Yukon Education, Queensland Department of Education and Training and New Zealand Ministry of Education (2016), Data Questionnaires.

Canadian jurisdictions have concerns about the accuracy of numbers (which depend on self-identification of Indigenous people) and the impact this may have on calculating enrolment rates. For example, self-identification rates in population surveys may differ from reports by parents to schools.

While it is very important for Canadian jurisdictions to continue to make progress on obtaining accurate information on the students in their province or territory, the existing data does appear to indicate that a significant number of Indigenous students are not in school – a critical and alarming issue. If this was not the case, the total enrolment rates for non-Indigenous and Indigenous students would exceed 100%, which they do not, as shown in Figure 5.5. In addition, the enrolment patterns across provinces and territories are remarkably similar, including over time, for those that have trend data.

The use of population surveys is the basis on which countries (including Canada) report student enrolment rates to the OECD. These are drawn from bodies responsible for national data. In Canada, this body is Statistics Canada. Population surveys are also used to calculate the prevalence of other outcomes, such as health indicators.

As noted previously, New Zealand is the only jurisdiction in this study that actively monitors student enrolment rates. This is done through the use of population surveys and enrolment numbers reported by schools.

In looking at where participation rates vary most between Indigenous and non-Indigenous students, Figure 5.5 shows that Indigenous students are more likely to enter education at a later age than other Canadian students. While the gap in the participation rates between Indigenous and non-Indigenous students declines as students get older, a significant gap remains throughout students' schooling years.

Figure 5.5. Participation rates of Indigenous and non-Indigenous students by age, 2015

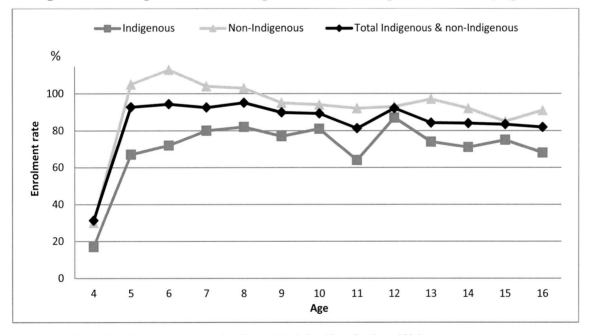

Note: In the figure, Canadian data include only Alberta, Manitoba, Nova Scotia and Yukon.

Sources: Alberta Education, Manitoba Education, Nova Scotia Education and Yukon Education (2016), Data Questionnaires.

In New Zealand, the participation patterns of Indigenous students differ from those in Canada. The extent of a later start in education is much smaller, and participation levels throughout schooling remain higher. However, retention at senior secondary schooling in New Zealand drops when students reach age 16, falling below the participation rate for Canadian Indigenous students at age 17 (Figure 5.6).

Figure 5.6. Participation rates of Indigenous students in Canada and New Zealand, 2015

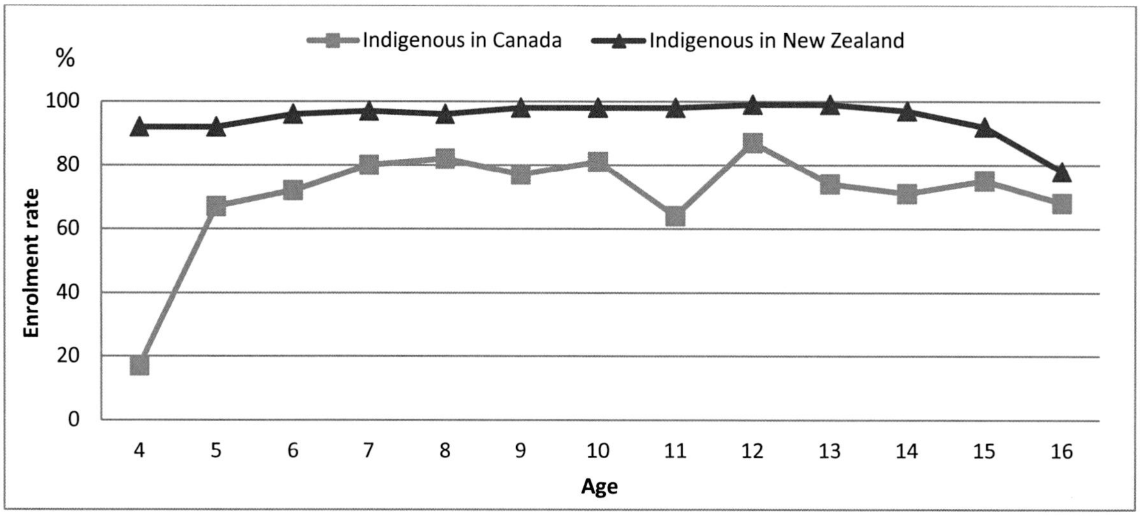

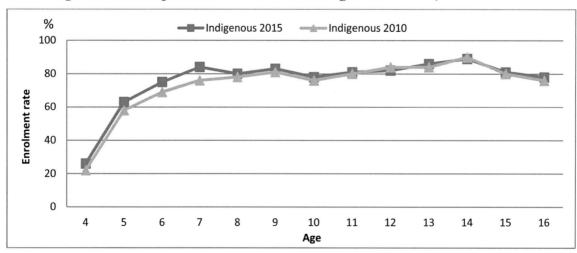

Note: In the figure, Canadian data include only Alberta, Manitoba, Nova Scotia and Yukon.

Sources: Alberta Education, Manitoba Education, Nova Scotia Education, Yukon Education and New Zealand Ministry of Education (2016), Data Questionnaires.

There are differences in practices across jurisdictions on the age at which children start school. For all the jurisdictions in this study, however, the mandatory age for starting school is 6.

Is the gap closing?

Only Alberta and Manitoba have Indigenous enrolment numbers for both 2010 and 2015.[5] Between 2010 and 2015, there have been slight improvements in enrolment rates in the early years. This is encouraging, but the data does not show improvements at other age levels, and there appear to be slight declines in participation rates at lower secondary levels (Figure 5.7).

Figure 5.7. Participation rates of Canadian Indigenous students, 2010 and 2015

Note: In the figure, Canadian data include only Alberta and Manitoba.

Sources: Alberta Education and Manitoba Education (2016), Data Questionnaires.

New Zealand achieved improvements in participation rates from 2005 to 2015. This is evident in an increase in early-years participation rates between 2010 and 2015.[6] More noteworthy, however, are the significant increases in participation rates from 2005 to 2015 for Indigenous students age 14-16 (Figure 5.8).

Figure 5.8. Participation rates of Indigenous students in New Zealand, 2005, 2010 and 2015

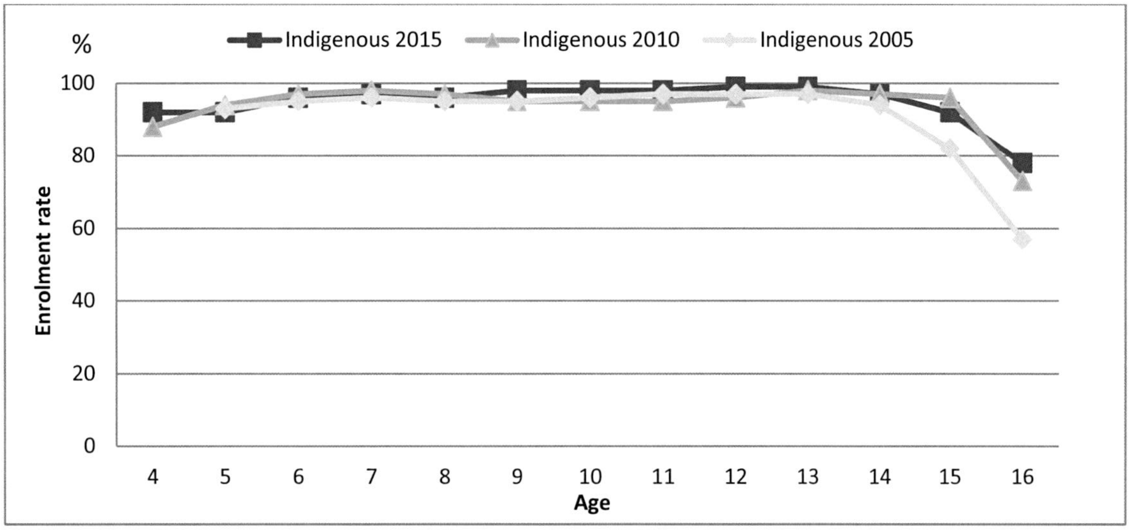

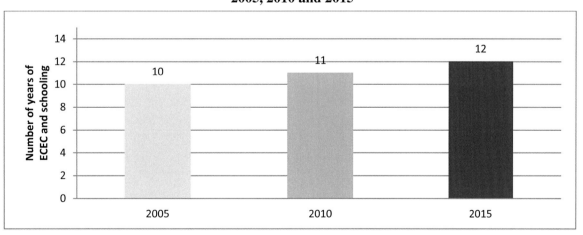

Source: New Zealand Ministry of Education (2016), Data Questionnaire.

The overall effect of rising Indigenous student enrolment rates in New Zealand has been an increase in the overall years of education that these students are now receiving, although non-Indigenous students in New Zealand still have one year more of basic education, on average.

Figure 5.9. Years of ECEC and schooling of Indigenous students in New Zealand, 2005, 2010 and 2015

Source: New Zealand Ministry of Education (2016), Data Questionnaire.

Figure 5.9 illustrates the incremental improvement that New Zealand has achieved from 2005 to 2015. But given the persistent efforts New Zealand has made to increase enrolment rates of Indigenous students, it underlines how long it can take to achieve visible progress.

Participation patterns by gender

Gender differences between students' participation patterns in ECEC and schooling in OECD countries are more commonly observed at senior levels of schooling than in the early or middle years. This is also true for Indigenous students in Canada, New Zealand and Queensland. For Indigenous children in the early years (age 4-7), the gender ratios are largely equivalent in the jurisdictions in this study. The participation rates of Indigenous boys and girls are the same in Alberta and New Brunswick, and there are proportionately slightly more boys in education than girls at these ages in New Zealand and Queensland.

During the middle schooling years (age 8-14), Indigenous boys and girls participate in schooling at equivalent rates in New Zealand and Queensland. In Alberta, Manitoba and New Brunswick, the participation rate of girls slightly exceeds that of boys.

In senior schooling, Indigenous girls are more likely to be in education than Indigenous boys in New Zealand, Nova Scotia and Queensland. The tendency for girls to more likely be in education than boys at age 15-18 is also found among non-Indigenous students in each of these jurisdictions. In contrast, Indigenous boys in New Brunswick are more likely than Indigenous girls to be enrolled in education at this age. In Alberta and Manitoba, the participation rates of Indigenous boys and girls are similar at this level of education.

Course enrolments

Providing course options for students can be an effective means to retain students in education (particularly in the senior schooling years) and to support ongoing educational achievement. Students may prefer to enrol in the same courses as their peers, and some students will opt for easier courses to improve their grades or chance of passing. However, where enrolment options do not lead to ongoing education pathways or meaningful qualifications, they can result in dead ends for students tracked into these options.

Across OECD countries, tracking students into courses with lower expectations and fewer ongoing pathways is associated with poorer student performance. These negative impacts are stronger the earlier tracking occurs. Delaying tracking for as long as possible is generally associated with better education outcomes for students.

In some Canadian schools, especially in rural or remote areas, access to academic courses at senior high school can be limited. Thus, students are often not able to undertake courses they may wish or need to take to enter further education. Alternatively, students face the options of either distance learning or moving to an urban centre.

Few Canadian jurisdictions hold information on Indigenous students' enrolment in different types of courses, such as academic versus vocational programmes. Queensland does track this information, revealing, for example, that Indigenous students are less likely to be enrolled in academic mathematics programmes than non-Indigenous students.

Queensland also tracks Indigenous students' take-up of mathematics. Based on Queensland's reported enrolment rates, Indigenous students in Alberta are more likely to be enrolled in academic mathematics programmes than those in Queensland. Indigenous students in Queensland are evenly split across academic and vocational mathematics programmes.

Socio-economic disadvantage

The effectiveness of any education system is, in part, reflected in how well education mitigates disadvantage (rather than exacerbating it). Some systems are clearly better than others in relation to socio-economic disadvantage, and some systems, including all three countries in this study, are better at integrating and helping migrant children to succeed. However, there is not yet sound evidence on which countries are making progress on mitigating the intergenerational impacts of colonialism on the education outcomes of Indigenous children.

Only New Zealand was able to provide data on Indigenous students by their socio-economic status (SES), although only for 4-year-olds. In New Zealand, participation rates for both Indigenous and non-Indigenous students increase with students' level of socio-economic advantage, although the rates for Indigenous students are lower than for non-Indigenous students at each age group. Participation rates for Indigenous students from advantaged backgrounds are significantly higher than for Indigenous students from low and average SES backgrounds, but still only match those of non-Indigenous students from average and low SES backgrounds.

Geographic location

In general, across countries participating in PISA, students who attend schools in rural areas tend to score at lower levels than students in schools in urban areas. The difference is particularly large when the performance of students in rural areas is compared to that of students in city schools. However, a sizable portion (two-thirds) of these differences reflect differences in the socio-economic status of the students (OECD, 2013).

Limited data was available from jurisdictions on Indigenous students in urban, rural and remote areas. Data on this was provided by Alberta, New Zealand and the Northwest Territories. In general, students living in rural and remote areas have lower participation rates than students in urban areas. These differences, however, are larger for Indigenous students than non-Indigenous students.

Remote communities have particular difficulties in providing learning opportunities for students, especially in schools' ability to recruit and retain qualified, effective teachers. This is particularly the case in fly-in communities, where teachers can feel very isolated.

Learning difficulties

Indigenous students are more likely than non-Indigenous students to be assessed as having learning difficulties in Canada (Figure 5.10). The impacts of such assessments on students vary. In cases where students are provided with effective support for their learning, the results can be positive. However, if having a learning difficulty means students are withdrawn from regular classroom instruction and face lower expectations, a less demanding curriculum and lower-quality teachers, this can have a very negative impact on them. This is particularly the case when linguistic differences or the effects of trauma, such as witnessing violence, are interpreted as lack of ability.

An issue of particular concern in relation to Indigenous students assessed as having learning difficulties in Canada is the extent to which the percentage of students regarded as having learning difficulties increases as students become older. This may reflect diagnoses that were not undertaken at earlier ages, but it may also reflect an interpretation of certain characteristics or behaviours as indicative of learning difficulties when that is not in fact the case. For example, boys and migrant[7] students are more likely to be assessed as having special learning needs than girls and non-migrant students. While some boys and some migrant children may have behavioural and linguistic differences that distinguish them from other students, these do not necessarily equate to learning difficulties.

Figure 5.10. Indigenous and non-Indigenous students assessed with learning difficulties in Canada, 2015

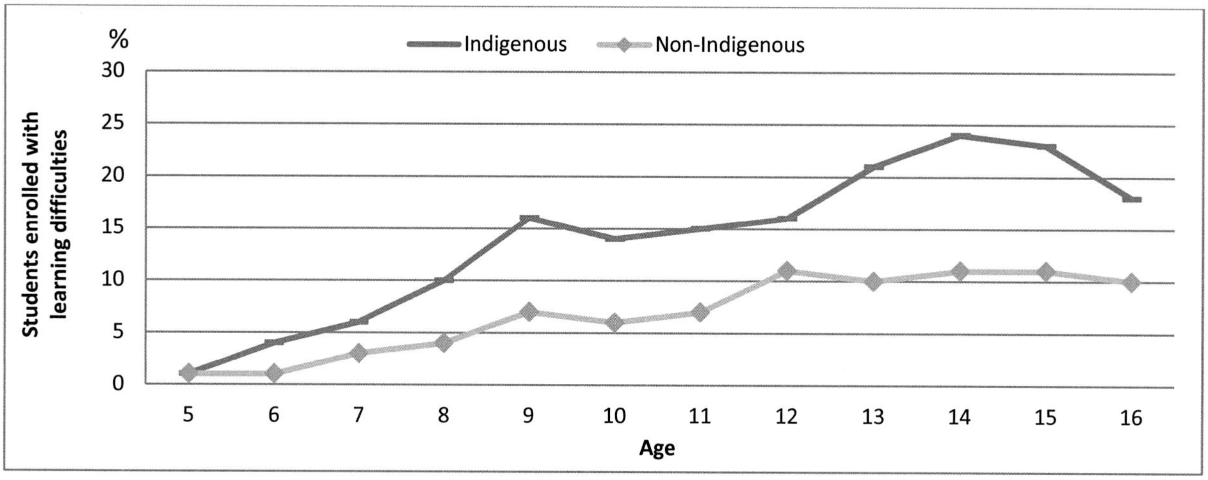

Note: In the figure, Canadian data include only Nova Scotia and Yukon.

Sources: Nova Scotia Education and Yukon Education Training (2016), Data Questionnaires.

Policies and practices to improve participation

The responsibility for students succeeding in education lies with the school systems responsible for these students. To improve outcomes for Indigenous students, school systems need to reorient to the needs and aspirations of these students and their families. Such reorientation needs to occur at the system level, in each local community, at every school, and between classroom teachers and individual Indigenous students and their families.

The key is to find the connection between the intent and commitment at the system level to support and enable positive change at the practitioner level. Across nearly every issue in education, school leadership is the crucial determinant of whether this connection occurs or not. However, the extent to which system-level actions enable and incentivise action at the local level impacts on both effectiveness and sustainability.

Policies that countries have used to improve early participation rates include:

Setting targets

- Participation targets at a national level have tended to focus on ECEC participation rates and senior school retention. Both New Zealand and Queensland have used this mechanism to communicate and mobilise action to achieve the target (Box 5.1). Australia, for example, has achieved significant improvements in Indigenous students' school completion rates, exceeding their target for 2015. Setting targets, however, needs to be accompanied by reliable data and monitoring. Alberta has made significant gains in this area through its Aboriginal Learner Data Collection Initiative, which has led to a better understanding of both Indigenous demographics and learner outcomes.

Box 5.1. Closing the Gap in Year 12 Certification

Queensland (Australia) has achieved significant and sustained improvements in the proportion of Indigenous students gaining Year 12 Certification (Queensland Certificate of Education [QCE] or Queensland Certificate of Individual Achievement [QCIA]). The QCE is a foundation-level, achievement-based qualification, which includes prescribed literacy and numeracy standards. The QCIA recognises the achievements of students who are on individualised learning programs. Without this basic level of competency, students struggle to access further education or employment and to achieve positive outcomes in other areas of their lives (Stanwick et al., 2014).

The following table sets out the rates for Indigenous and non-Indigenous students in state schools in Queensland since 2008. Note that improvements have been achieved for both groups of students.

Year	Indigenous Certification (%)	Non-Indigenous Certification (%)	Gap (percentage points)
2008	42.1	71.3	29.2
2009	49.1	74.3	25.2
2010	53.8	78.3	24.5
2011	65.9	82.5	16.6
2012	70.2	85.3	15.2
2013	75.9	89.1	13.2
2014	86.5	93.3	6.9
2015	95.0	96.9	1.8
2016	97.0	97.8	0.9

Source: Queensland Curriculum and Assessment Authority, 2017.

A Queensland Government reform programme to close the gap was the impetus for aligned changes in practices at the central, regional and school levels. The Department of Education's central office provided disaggregated data to each region, quantifying the number of Indigenous students needed to close the gap. This helped regions to see the objective in more concrete and achievable terms. For example, one region found that if 34 at-risk Indigenous students attained the QCE, the gap would be closed. Central office efforts also included workshops and leadership sessions for school leaders and regional staff to focus on why improvements were needed and how these might be realised.

Queensland's seven educational regions supported schools to achieve progress in a number of ways. One initiative has been the appointment of QCE coaches, who provide schools with profiles of on-risk students and access to funding to provide additional support for students, such as catch-up camps during school holidays.

Individual schools established multidisciplinary case-management teams to support to students, used student-achievement tracking systems, provided students with intensive teaching and learning opportunities, such as after-school tutoring, and held information sessions with parents on how to help their children succeed.

The significant improvements have been attributed to:

- alignment across schools, regional offices and central office in purposeful, consistent and deliberate efforts
- a clear line of sight to individual schools and students, by name
- intensive case management, to put in place "whatever it takes" to achieve success for each student.

Source: Button S. et al. (2016), "Whatever it takes: Year 12 Certification in Queensland", *Australian Educational Leader*, Vol. 38, No. 4, pp. 28-32.

Providing financial incentives

- Financial incentives to encourage families to enrol their children include targeting free provision of ECEC to disadvantaged children at early ages, universal free provision of ECEC, and transfer payments to low-income families for enrolling their children in school at the age of school entry.

- In remote communities in Queensland, Indigenous students who wish to pursue secondary education at urban schools can be assisted with scholarships and grants. These not only cover the direct costs of their participation in secondary school, but also provide ongoing support and guidance to assist students to adjust to their new schooling environment and continue until they complete their studies.

Using regulation

- Some jurisdictions use regulations to lower the compulsory age of entry to the education system and increase the school-leaving age.

Leading at the local level

- In the Canadian jurisdictions in this study, relationships have been built and agreements reached between on-reserve communities and provincial schools to ensure that all students from the on-reserve communities are enrolled and that the transitional phase and ongoing responsibility for each student is shared. This model works and is a promising practice led by committed Indigenous community leaders and education leaders.

Providing responsive, relevant services

- Provision of culturally appropriate services includes locating services within the target communities and recruiting and training staff from the target communities.

- Mobile services can be used to access remote and other hard-to-reach communities, where there are limited or no facilities.

- Teen parenting programmes are necessary to ensure the ongoing participation of students who become young parents.

- Targeted measures to prevent dropout can include diversifying opportunities to obtain an upper secondary qualification, with a range of pathways (including work-based training and/or certification based on a range of subjects and abilities) and providing incentives to stay in school until completion.

- The Northwest Territories is currently piloting a video-linked distance-learning programme for senior students in particular subjects. The programme is interactive between students and their teacher, connects students to other distance-learning students, and offers in-person support for students from an education support worker.

Targeting support

- Providing effective guidance, counselling and support mechanisms supports students to make well-informed choices in upper secondary education and in their transitions to further studies or the labour market.

- The Australian Indigenous Mentoring Experience programme, established in 2005, focuses on the retention of Indigenous students in senior schooling. The programme assigns university students as mentors for Indigenous high school students and offers internships, academic support and coaching in addition to mentoring.

Communications

- Campaigns within target communities to increase enrolment rates can include providing information to parents about the importance of students' participation in education and working with individual families to remove barriers to participation, including measures such as enrolment procedures, transport, clothing and food. Both New Zealand and Queensland have put in place campaigns to increase participation in ECEC by disadvantaged children, including Indigenous children.

Monitoring

- Transition programmes ensure that children and young people do not slip out of the system as they transition from one part of the education system to another or move to another centre or school in a different location.

- Student identifiers enable education systems to track, monitor and take action in relation to individual students' participation in education. New Zealand, for example, has introduced an early-learning information system that assigns each child a unique identifier, enabling student enrolment to be tracked from the first time a child enters the education system, from ECEC onwards (Box 5.2).

Box 5.2. Increasing participation rates in early childhood education

New Zealand has been increasing participation rates in early childhood education and care over a number of years. In 2012, the government set a Better Public Service goal to increase ECEC participation to 98% by December 2016. The table below shows the progress for Indigenous and non-Indigenous children over the last 15 years, noting the accelerated increases since 2012.

Year	Indigenous participation rate (%)	Total participation rate (%)	Gap (percentage points)
2002	84.8	91.2	6.4
2004	87.5	93.0	5.5
2006	88.1	93.4	5.3
2008	88.7	93.6	4.9
2010	89.6	94.3	4.7
2012	90.9	94.9	4.0
2014	92.9	95.9	3.0
2016	95.0	96.7	1.7

Source: Ministry of Education in New Zealand (2017), https://education.govt.nz/ministry-of-education/.

Box 5.2. Increasing participation rates in early childhood education *(continued)*

In 2012, the Ministry of Education established an Early Learning Task Force to implement the Better Public Service goal on ECEC participation rates. To achieve this level of increase, the Task Force needed to focus on groups of children with relatively lower participation rates, notably Māori and children of Pacific Island descent. The Task Force has used a data-focused methodology, setting regional targets for the number of children in communities that needed to be engaged. Its work has four key strands:

1. Partnering with Māori and Pasifika communities to understand and co-construct solutions to address gaps in provision and improve quality in children's early learning.

2. Seeking support from the broad community, including churches, employers, sports clubs and social service groups.

3. Working with other government agencies, including the Ministries of Social Development, Health, Pacific Island Affairs and *Te Puni Kōkiri* (Māori Development).

4. Working with schools in low socio-economic areas to identify and reach children who are not participating in ECEC.

Engaging Priority Families (EPF) Co-ordinators were established to support the hardest-to-reach families to enrol their children in ECEC, attend regularly, undertake learning activities at home and transition effectively to school.

Funding is also provided through grants, incentives and partnerships to provide new ECEC places in targeted communities. From 2012 to 2016, this programme provided 166 grants and created over 6 200 new ECEC places for high-priority families.

Source: Ministry of Education in New Zealand (2017), https://education.govt.nz/ministry-of-education/.

Notes

1. In New Zealand, the definition used is the number of students attending state or state-integrated schools as a proportion of all students at each age. For Queensland, the definition used is the number of students attending state and private schools as a proportion of all students at each age.

2. See Chapter 6 for information on attendance levels of enrolled students.

3. The number of years of basic education represents the number of years for which at least 90% of the population of school age are enrolled.

4. Data from New Brunswick and the Northwest Territories are not included.

5. The Northwest Territories has individual enrolment numbers for 2010, but as clarification is pending on some issues, it was not possible to include those data.

6. Recording of participation rates of 4-year-olds in ECEC commenced in New Zealand in 2009. Data prior to 2009 are not available.

7. Migrant students are defined as students whose parents were foreign-born.

References

Barro, R. and J. W. Lee (2013), "A new data set of educational attainment in the World, 1950-2010", *Journal of Development Economics,* Vol. 104, pp. 184-198, www.nber.org/papers/w15902.

Bartik, T. J. (2014), *From Preschool to Prosperity: The Economic Payoff to Early Childhood Education*, W.E. Upjohn Institute for Employment Research, Kalamazoo, www.upjohn.org/sites/default/files/WEfocus/FromPreschooltoProsperity.pdf.

Button S. et al. (2016), "Whatever it takes: Year 12 Certification in Queensland", *Australian Educational Leader*, Vol. 38, No. 4, pp. 28-32.

Duncan, G. J. and K. Magnuson (2013), "Investing in Preschool Programs" *Journal of Economic Perspectives,* 27 (2), www.aeaweb.org/articles?id=10.1257/jep.27.2.109.

Duncan, G.J. and A.J. Soujourner (2013), "Can Intensive Early Childhood Intervention Programs Eliminate Income-Based Cognitive and Achievement Gaps?", *Journal of Human Resources*, 48(4), 945-968, http://pubmedcentralcanada.ca/pmcc/articles/PMC4302948/.

Lleras-Muney, A. (2002), "Were compulsory attendance and child labor laws effective? An analysis from 1915 to 1939", *Journal of Law and Economics*, Vol. 45/2, pp. 401-435, www.nber.org/papers/w8563.

Oreopoulos, P. (2006). "The Compelling Effects of Compulsory Schooling: Evidence from Canada", *Canadian Journal of Economics/Revue canadienne d'économique,* Vol. 39/1, pp. 22-52, http://oreopoulos.faculty.economics.utoronto.ca/wp-content/uploads/2014/03/The-Compelling-Effects-of-Compulsory-Schooling.pdf.

OECD (forthcoming), *Early Learning*, OECD Publishing, Paris.

OECD (2016a), PISA 2015 Database, www.oecd.org/pisa/data/2015database/.

OECD (2016b), *Education at a Glance 2016: OECD Indicators*, OECD Publishing, Paris, http://dx.doi.org/10.1787/eag-2016-en.

OECD (2015), *Education Policy Outlook 2015: Making Reforms Happen,* OECD Publishing, Paris, http://dx.doi.org/10.1787/9789264225442-en.

OECD (2013), *PISA 2012 Results: Excellence through Equity (Volume II): Giving Every Student the Chance to Succeed,* PISA, OECD Publishing, Paris, http://dx.doi.org/10.1787/9789264201132-en.

OECD (2012), *Equity and Quality in Education: Supporting Disadvantaged Students and Schools,* OECD Publishing, Paris, http://dx.doi.org/10.1787/9789264130852-en.

Stanwick J. et al. (2014), *How young people are faring in the transition from school to work*, Foundation for Young Australians, Sydney, www.voced.edu.au/content/ngv%3A66025.

Sylva, K. et al. (2004). The Effective Provision of Pre-School Education (EPPE) Project: Final Report, Department for Education and Skills, Nottingham, http://webarchive. nationalarchives.gov.uk/20130401151715/https:/www.education.gov.uk/publications/s tandard/publicationDetail/Page1/SSU/FR/2004/01.

Queensland Curriculum and Assessment Authority (2017), www.qcaa.qld.edu.au/.

Chapter 6

Improving the engagement of Indigenous students in education

While improving students' well-being and ensuring participation of all students are the first steps to improve student outcomes, student engagement plays a crucial role. Engagement in education is a necessary precondition for student learning so that students can develop their skills and enjoy education. Better understanding how to improve student engagement can help support students to remain in education and do well at it. This chapter investigates the role of student engagement in education and the indicators that reflect it. The analysis explores evidence on student engagement and identifies promising policies and practices to improve it. Recognition and integration of Indigenous values and approaches are critical for achieving improvements in this area.

The statistical data for Israel are supplied by and under the responsibility of the relevant Israeli authorities. The use of such data by the OECD is without prejudice to the status of the Golan Heights, East Jerusalem and Israeli settlements in the West Bank under the terms of international law.

While the first steps in improving education outcomes are to improve student well-being and ensure participation of all students, students must also actively engage in the processes of learning to develop their skills. There are many reasons why students may not engage in learning or school generally, and there is also a wide range of actions that can increase the likelihood that students will engage. Understanding student engagement can help to better support students who are not achieving their potential or who are at risk of underachieving.

Little active monitoring of student engagement is occurring at a system level across most of the Canadian jurisdictions in this study, in terms of either positive or negative indicators of engagement. New Zealand and Queensland, however, both monitor Indigenous students' absenteeism and expulsions.

This chapter investigates the role of students' engagement in education in their well-being and educational achievement, explores evidence on engagement and identifies promising policies and practices to improve it.

Why engagement matters

The process of learning is voluntary and internal. It takes engagement and motivation to learn (Christenson, Reschly and Wylie, 2012). Students' attitudes towards learning, as well as their behaviour in and out of school, have a considerable impact on their performance. This includes the amount of time and effort students invest in learning and students' perseverance and motivation in completing their schoolwork. Thus, student engagement is a necessary, but not entirely sufficient, condition for positive student learning and development.

The OECD evidence base, through the Programme for International Student Assessment (PISA), finds that high-performing students have greater perseverance, motivation and self-confidence than students who do not perform so well. Students who do not do well are more likely to skip classes or days of school, arrive late for school and do less homework than higher-performing students. For example, students who had skipped an entire school day at least once in the two weeks prior to the PISA test in 2012 were almost three times more likely to score at a low level in mathematics than students who did not skip school (more than twice as likely after accounting for students' socio-economic status, gender, immigrant background and attendance at pre-primary education).

By playing truant, students miss out on learning opportunities, increase the likelihood of dropping out of school entirely and limit their lifetime employment opportunities. However, being physically present at school is not enough. Without perseverance, motivation and self-esteem, students may struggle to make the most of available opportunities, regardless of their aptitude.

Students' sense of self-efficacy (the extent to which they believe in their own ability to solve specific tasks) and self-concept (their beliefs in their own abilities) have a considerable impact on their self-confidence, perseverance and motivation, and ultimately on their performance in school (Schunk and Pajares, 2009). Students who lack self-confidence in their ability to complete particular tasks may wrongly assume that investing more effort is a waste of time. In a self-fulfilling prophecy, this leads to less engagement at school and poorer performance (OECD, 2013a).

Students' attitudes towards school and learning are important well beyond their influence on academic success. Feeling safe, socially connected and happy at school are ends in themselves, especially since school is a primary venue for students' social development. The importance of these aspects of school life is reflected in the priority parents give to a pleasant, active and safe environment when choosing a school for their child (OECD, 2015) and in the strong consensus among teachers that the social and emotional development of students is as important as their acquisition of knowledge and skills (OECD, 2013a).

It is vital for education systems to understand the role that student attitudes play in learning, particularly for students who are disadvantaged in some way. Fostering positive attitudes can result in significant improvements in performance at little cost (Dweck, 2006). The value of greater student engagement, perseverance, motivation and self-confidence cannot be overstated.

For students, there are two ways to improve academic performance: invest more time and effort (behavioural) and/or reduce levels of anxiety (affective). Both of these strategies require some changes in students' beliefs and self-beliefs. For example, improving students' confidence in their abilities, knowledge and skills, and instilling in them the conviction that success is the result of hard work (not of innate and fixed traits) (Dweck, 2006) or the belief that academic success leads to professional success can help to reduce anxiety and foster motivation (Schunk and Pajares, 2009). When students feel they belong at school, they are also more motivated. The virtuous circle is complete, because students invest more of their time and effort in their schoolwork when they are motivated.

Indicators of engagement

The OECD has used several measures to capture levels of student engagement and the relationships of these measures with students' academic performance. The two behaviours that impact most on students' academic performance relative to PISA are absenteeism and lack of punctuality. Students who skipped class or days of school in the two weeks prior to the PISA test in 2015 scored, on average, 45 points lower in science than students who did not skip classes or school (33 points lower after accounting for the socio-economic profile of students and schools). Students who reported that they arrived late for school in the two weeks before they sat the PISA test scored, on average, 27 points lower than students who reported they had been punctual (23 points lower after accounting for the socio-economic profile of students and schools).

The impact on students who arrive late for school and skip classes or days of school is that they are not gaining the learning opportunities they need. Students who are disadvantaged or who are struggling with their learning need more rather than fewer opportunities to develop and learn. In addition, students' absenteeism and lack of punctuality can have a disruptive effect on their classmates and their school. This can be particularly problematic for schools that have high proportions of students who demonstrate these behaviours.

Absenteeism

Absenteeism is a problem in many countries. Across OECD countries, 26% of students reported that they had skipped at least one class, and 20% reported that they had skipped an entire day of school without authorisation in the two weeks before the PISA test. As noted above, across OECD countries, the difference in science performance associated with skipping classes or days of school is 45 score points.

The percentage of Canadian students who skip school is around 18%, just under the OECD average of 20%. New Zealand is well over the average, with a rate of 25%, and Australia reaches 29%. Skipping class is more common among disadvantaged students than among advantaged students in all three countries (Figure 6.1) (OECD, 2016a).

Canadian students who do not do well on PISA are, on average, more likely to have skipped school at least once in the two weeks prior to the 2012 PISA test than low performers in other countries (31.6% of low-performing Canadian students reported doing so, compared to the OECD average of 22.6%). The rate was 44.5% for Australia and 35.1% for New Zealand. For all three countries, there is a strong association between active disengagement from school and poor performance (OECD, 2016b).

Figure 6.1. Percentage of students who skip days of school, 2012 and 2015

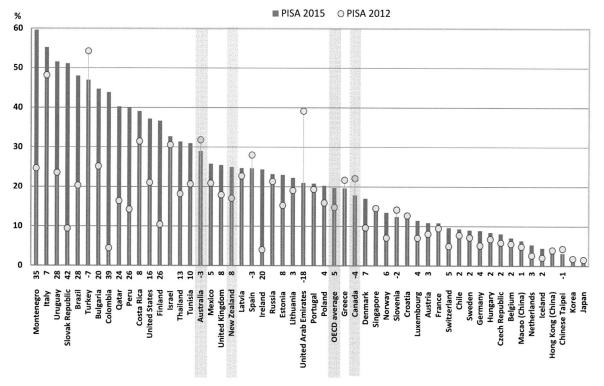

Note: Percentage of students who reported that they skipped a day of school at least once in the two weeks prior to the PISA test. Only countries/economies that participated in both 2012 and 2015 PISA assessments are shown. Only percentage-point difference between PISA 2012 and PISA 2015 that are statistically significant are shown next to the country/economy name (see Annex A3 of OECD, 2016a).

Countries and economies are ranked in descending order of the percentage of students who had skipped a whole day of school at least once in the two weeks prior to the PISA test in 2015.

Source: OECD (2016a), PISA 2015 Database, Tables II.3.1, II.3.2 and II.3.3, www.oecd.org/pisa/data/2015database/.

StatLink ⫶⫶⫶ http://dx.doi.org/10.1787/888933435655.

There are, however, reasons other than engagement that lead students to be absent from school. For example, ill health of students themselves or of other family members is an obvious reason for absence. The need to attend significant events (such as funerals) may affect some groups of students more than others. For students in remote areas, medical or other appointments in the nearest urban centre can result in an absence of several days.

Wherever possible, a distinction should be made between explained and unexplained absences, although both should be monitored for individual students at the school level. What is important is that schools understand what lies behind student absences, and that action be taken to mitigate the negative impacts of such absences on students' opportunities for success.

Punctuality

In 2015, significant proportions of students had arrived late for school, without authorisation, at least once in the two weeks prior to the PISA test. On average across OECD countries, almost one in two students (44%) reported having arrived late at least once during that two-week period (Figure 6.2). The percentage is higher, on average, for students from disadvantaged backgrounds (47%) than for those from advantaged backgrounds (43%).

As for skipping class, arriving late for school was more predictive of mathematics performance and was lower than the OECD average in Australia, Canada and New Zealand. For students from disadvantaged backgrounds in Australia, Canada and New Zealand, this performance penalty was higher than the OECD average. Disadvantaged students in Australia, Canada and New Zealand were also more likely to arrive late for school than disadvantaged students in other countries. In New Zealand, more than one in two socio-economically disadvantaged students reported having arrived late for school at least once in the two weeks before the PISA test.

Lack of punctuality may be associated with socio-economic disadvantage for a range of reasons. In some countries, disadvantaged students may have no private means of transportation to school and may need to use public transport or be responsible for getting themselves to school, even at a young age. Where there is public transport, it may not always operate in a regular or reliable fashion. Disadvantaged students may also have more responsibilities than advantaged students, such as the need to look after younger siblings and other family members and to undertake paid work before or after school.

Reductions were achieved in the overall proportion of students arriving late at school between 2003 and 2015 in the three countries in this study. However, these improvements were largely among advantaged rather than disadvantaged students (OECD, 2016b).

Figure 6.2. Percentage of students who arrive late for school, 2015

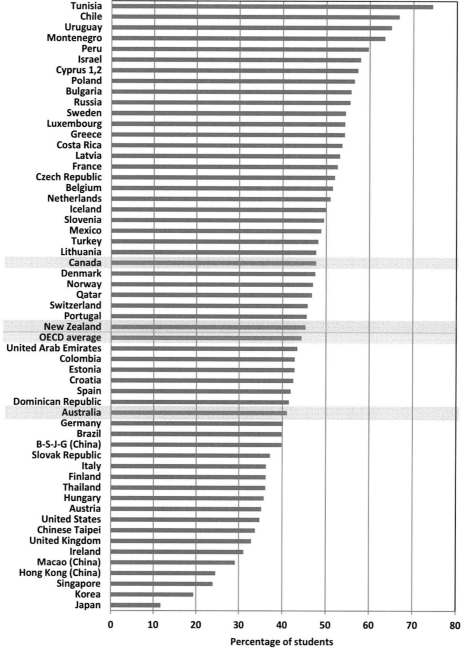

Notes: Percentage of students who reported that they had arrived late for school at least once or twice during the two weeks prior to the PISA test. Argentina, Kazakhstan and Malaysia were not included in this figure, as coverage is too small to ensure comparability (see Annex A4 of OECD, 2016a).

1. Footnote by Turkey: The information in this document with reference to « Cyprus » relates to the southern part of the Island. There is no single authority representing both Turkish and Greek Cypriot people on the Island. Turkey recognises the Turkish Republic of Northern Cyprus (TRNC). Until a lasting and equitable solution is found within the context of the United Nations, Turkey shall preserve its position concerning the "Cyprus issue".

2. Footnote by all the European Union Member States of the OECD and the European Union: The Republic of Cyprus is recognised by all members of the United Nations with the exception of Turkey. The information in this document relates to the area under the effective control of the Government of the Republic of Cyprus.

Countries and economies are ranked in descending order of the percentage of students who arrived late, at least once or twice during the two weeks prior to the PISA test.

Source: OECD, PISA 2015 Database (Vol II), Table II.3.1, http://dx.doi.org/10.1787/888933436489.

Homework

Academic performance is strongly associated with time spent on homework. On average across OECD countries, students who reported devoting more time to homework were less likely to perform below the baseline level of proficiency in mathematics, even after accounting for socio-economic status, gender, immigrant background and attendance at pre-primary education. Spending one hour per week on homework is associated with a 15% reduction in the probability of scoring poorly in mathematics, compared to doing no homework. Devoting two hours per week on homework is associated with a 36% reduction in that likelihood, and three hours per week is associated with a 50% reduction. The probability of scoring poorly continues to decrease as the number of hours spent on homework increases, but only up to a point, after which there are nil returns on the investment (OECD, 2016c).

There are many reasons why students invest relatively low levels of time on homework. They can include the lack of a suitable, quiet place at home to study, the need to contribute to family and other activities, inadequate parental guidance or supervision in students' younger years, lack of confidence in their ability to understand or complete the homework, and lack of interest in the task and/or subject matter. This last issue is particularly important when curriculum material or education tasks have little relevance or meaning to groups within the student population, including Indigenous students (Young, 2010).

In both Canada and Australia, low-performing students spend about the same number of hours on homework as low performers in many other countries (close to the OECD average for low performers of 3.5 hours). Compared to other students in their own countries, all three groups of low performers undertake less homework each week, and this indicator is particularly pronounced among low performers in Australia (Figure 6.3).

Figure 6.3. Hours spent doing homework, low and high performers in mathematics, 2012

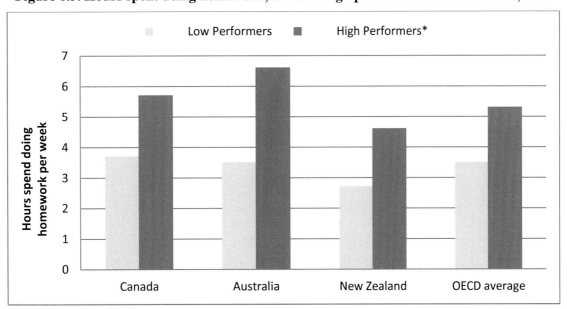

Note: High performers are students scoring above the baseline Level 2 in mathematics.
Source: OECD (2016a), PISA 2015 Database, www.oecd.org/pisa/data/2015database/.

Concentration and effort

Students who do not perform well in PISA report that they find it difficult to concentrate fully on the task at hand. In most countries, these students are less likely than better-performing students to report that they pay attention or listen in mathematics class.

Students who perform at lower levels also report applying less effort than their higher-performing peers, even in the PISA test itself. This difference among students is significant in all three countries participating in this study. While students who felt that they performed badly on the test might be reluctant to accept that they had invested the same effort as other students, these figures offer yet another indication that students who struggle with mathematics may not be applying themselves fully in academic activities.

Progress in monitoring engagement

Monitoring indicators of disengagement of Indigenous students does not appear to be common across the six Canadian jurisdictions in this study, although Nova Scotia and Yukon do have information on the absence rates of Indigenous students during 2015.

No Canadian jurisdiction recorded expulsions or exclusions of Indigenous students,[1] while both New Zealand and Queensland monitored these rates from 2005-15 and 2010-15.

Patterns in engagement

Absenteeism is a significant issue for Indigenous students in the jurisdictions that reported on this indicator. While absenteeism can reflect a range of issues in students' lives, including disengagement from school, it negatively impacts on these students' opportunities for learning and their likely success in education.

Student absences

Based on data from Nova Scotia and Yukon, we can see that absence rates for all students increase as they get older. At all ages, however, Indigenous students have a higher propensity to be absent than non-Indigenous students, and this gap widens from age 13 onwards. The impact on individual students is that they have access to fewer opportunities to learn than non-Indigenous students and are at risk of not being able to make sound educational progress. This leads to lower motivation and increased disengagement.

At the schools we visited, the biggest challenge teachers raised in relation to Indigenous student achievement was the amount of time students spent away from school. Teachers we met at a high school with a relatively high proportion of Indigenous students estimated that most Indigenous students were only at school three to four days a week, compared to an average of four to five days for non-Indigenous students. While some schools appeared to have active and effective strategies to address this, others did not.

Figure 6.4. Days absent of Indigenous and non-Indigenous students in Canada, 2015

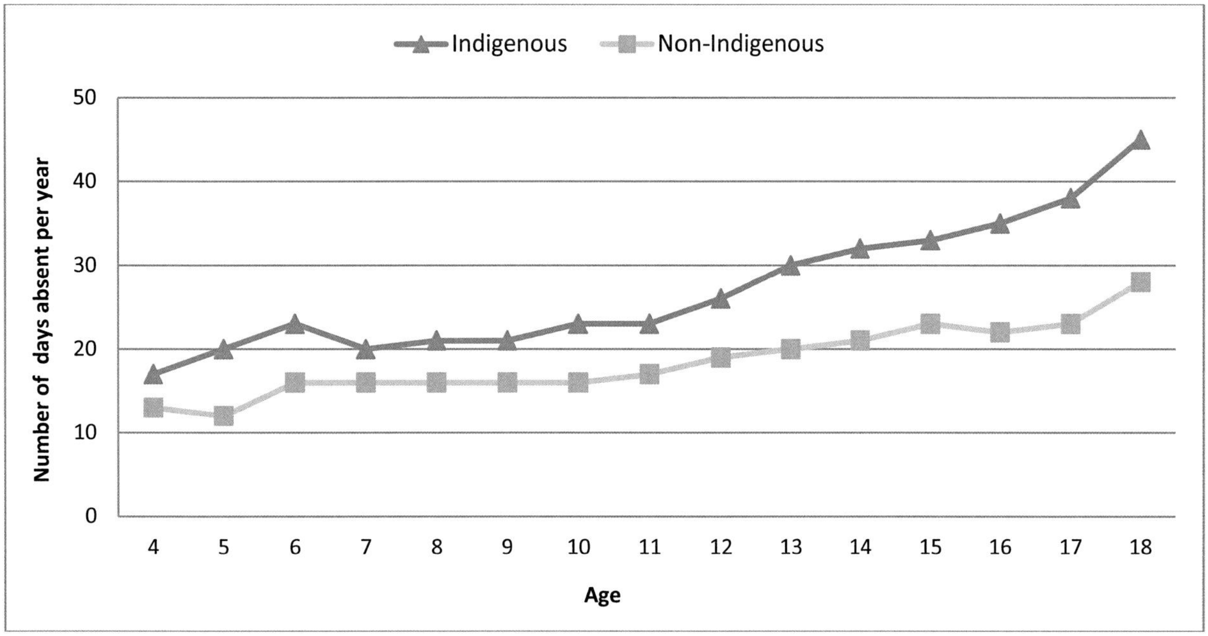

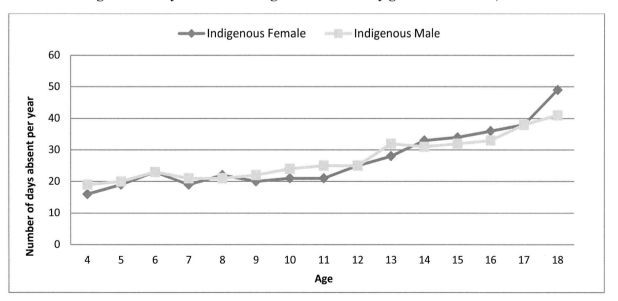

Note: In the figure, Canadian data include only Nova Scotia and Yukon.

Sources: Nova Scotia Education and Yukon Education (2016), Data Questionnaires.

There are fewer differences between individual students on the basis of gender (Figure 6.5). Girls are slightly more at risk of being absent in the earlier years, boys more so in the middle years, and then girls are absent more frequently in the senior years of schooling.

Figure 6.5. Days absent of Indigenous students by gender in Canada, 2015

Note: In the figure, Canadian data include only Nova Scotia and Yukon.

Sources: Nova Scotia Education and Yukon Education (2016), Data Questionnaires.

Compared to New Zealand and Queensland, Indigenous students in Nova Scotia and Yukon are much more likely to be absent from school. In addition, the increased risk of absenteeism amongst Indigenous students in older age groups is much less pronounced in Queensland (Figure 6.6).

Figure 6.6. Days absent of Indigenous students in Canada, New Zealand and Queensland, 2015

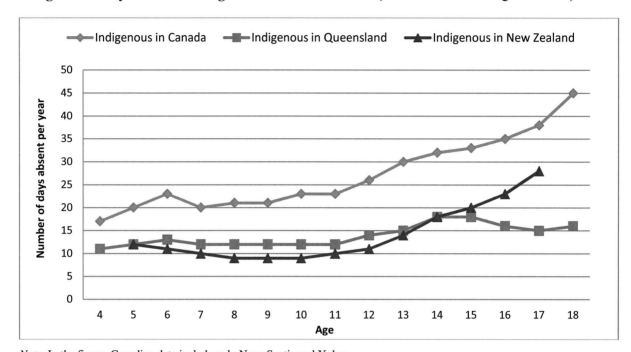

Note: In the figure, Canadian data include only Nova Scotia and Yukon.

Sources: Nova Scotia Education, Yukon Education, Queensland Department of Education and Training and New Zealand Ministry of Education (2016), Data Questionnaires.

Expulsions

Expulsion from school has extreme consequences for students, severely limiting their ability to successfully complete school and gain the skills and qualifications they need to enter the labour market or further education. Behaviours that result in expulsion are often symptomatic of deep emotional issues that have existed for some time and have not been effectively addressed. Sometimes students act out to get the attention they need or, in some cases, students are simply not aware of the potential implications of their behaviour.

Rules vary hugely across systems, and how the rules are applied is often a matter of judgement by teachers and education leaders. Teachers and school principals may have greater empathy for students they can identify with than for other groups of students, and therefore may apply discretionary rules differently.

None of the Canadian jurisdictions participating in this study provided data on expulsions[2] and exclusions[3], but such data was provided by New Zealand (Figure 6.7).

Indigenous students in New Zealand are more likely to be excluded or expelled than non-Indigenous students. In New Zealand, this gap is most pronounced among students from age 11 to age 16.

Figure 6.7. Expulsion rates of Indigenous students in New Zealand, 2015, 2010 and 2005

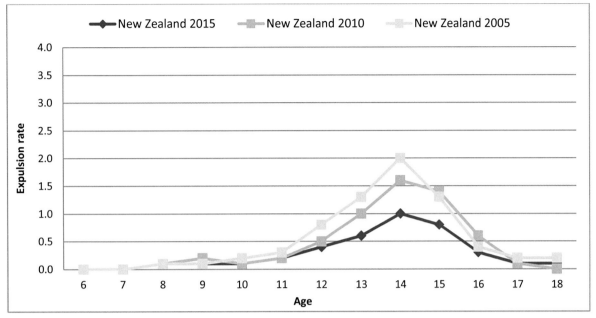

Source: New Zealand Ministry of Education (2016), Data Questionnaire.

Policies and practices to improve engagement

Policies and practices that support the engagement of Indigenous students in education and learning are set out below, with examples drawn from across participating jurisdictions. While each policy and practice is likely to have some positive effect on Indigenous students, no single policy or practice is likely to be sufficient to make notable improvements in the engagement of Indigenous students. Rather, it is the combined impact of a tailored set of responses that will be effective. Schools visited for this study that had high levels of engagement among Indigenous students were using a combination of the following practices and policies:

Visibility of Indigenous cultures in schools and classrooms

The visibility of Indigenous cultures in schools and classrooms respects and recognises the importance of the Indigenous peoples of Canada. Schools can support the engagement of Indigenous students by providing environments where Indigenous students feel connected to their culture and valued for their heritage.

An easy action for schools to take is to use signage at the entrance of the school that is symbolic of Indigenous cultures and includes the use of an Indigenous language or languages. Such symbols should not be superficial; they should be integrated into the school ethos and learning activities.

In the Northwest Territories, the need to construct a new school building provided an opportunity to take a new approach. Indigenous cultural symbolism is integrated throughout the school, offering opportunities to learn about Indigenous culture and Northwest Territory history and providing modern, comfortable spaces for students to learn in.

In some cases, school leaders will have to hold their ground in the face of resistance to such changes from some non-Indigenous parents. In one school we visited, the principal was dealing with a campaign by non-Indigenous parents who oppose the installation of a smudging facility on the school grounds. Our overall impression from our visits to schools, however, was that there are very high levels of interest by non-Indigenous students in learning about Canadian Indigenous cultures.

Adopting Indigenous cultural practices

The use of culturally appropriate practices in everyday school life is also an effective way to value Indigenous students and their families. We saw first-hand the powerfully positive effect of smudging on Indigenous and non-Indigenous students in a school environment.

A number of schools use talking circles as a way of connecting with students and of resolving issues. In some cases, Elders and parents are involved, including where there has been conflict between Indigenous and non-Indigenous students. Such processes have reportedly had positive, sustained impacts for both groups of students.

A high school in Alberta holds eagle-feather ceremonies at student graduations. Indigenous children from local elementary schools are invited to these ceremonies to help them to see that success at the end of schooling is a reality they can achieve.

An example from New Zealand is that of *Te Whakatika*. This is a process of helping students to resolve and make amends for wrongdoing, similar to contemporary restorative justice group conferencing (Hooper et al., 1999). This is a more effective and much less damaging alternative to punishment, such as suspending[4] or excluding students.

Some of the schools we visited ensure that students have the opportunity to experience powwows and sweat lodges. A school in Manitoba that has achieved significant improvements in Indigenous student outcomes uses sweat lodges as a way for teachers to learn about local Indigenous culture and for staff and students to be more connected. A teacher at this school talked to us about her experience of sweat lodges and how such experiences help to create strong connections between staff and Indigenous students. She commented: "We're like a family. Staff are investing in the children, and the children can feel it."

Including Indigenous histories and cultures in the curriculum

Schools that most successfully embed Indigenous perspectives into the curriculum are those that integrate Indigenous history, science and philosophy into all courses, for the benefit of all students. Nova Scotia, for example, has recently integrated Treaty Education into the compulsory curriculum from Grade 1 to Grade 6. The Indigenous leaders we met on the field visits were highly supportive of such developments. As the Truth and Reconciliation Commission noted, it is essential for all Canadians to understand this critical part of their history (Truth and Reconciliation Commission, 2015).

The Australian Curriculum mandates that Aboriginal and Torres Strait Islander histories and cultures are a cross-curriculum priority. This means that Indigenous perspectives need to be embedded across the curriculum and that all students engage in reconciliation and recognition of the Indigenous identities and cultures.[5]

Using curriculum resources developed by and reflecting Indigenous peoples

A very easy step for schools to take is to provide and use books and other resources developed by Indigenous people. For example, contemporary texts by Indigenous authors can be integrated as curriculum resources.

Show Me Your Math is a programme developed by researchers at the Faculty of Education at Saint Francis Xavier University in Antigonish, Nova Scotia (Box 6.1). The programme supports teachers and students to explore mathematics in their own community and cultural practices. Through exploring aspects of counting, measuring, locating, designing, playing and explaining, students discover that mathematics is all around them. Every year, students gather for an annual mathematics fair to share and celebrate the work they have done.

Box 6.1. Engaging Indigenous students in math

Show Me Your Math

 In Nova Scotia, the late Mi'kmaw Elder and quillbox maker, Dianne Toney, explained that to make a ring for a circular box top, she measured three times across the circle with her wood strips and added a thumb width. She declared that it makes a perfect circle every time. This conversation with Dr. Lisa Lunney Borden and Dr. David Wagner prompted the two to consider how Mi'kmaw children might enter into such conversations with Elders in their own communities.

Working with teachers and Elders in *Mi'kmaw Kina'matnewey* community schools, Borden and Wagner developed the Show Me Your Math programme. Show Me Your Math is a programme that invites Aboriginal Students in Atlantic Canada to explore the mathematics that is evident in their own community and cultural practices. Through exploring aspects of counting, measuring, locating, designing, playing, and explaining, students discover that mathematics is all around them and is connected to many of the cultural practices in their own communities. Each year students gather for the annual math fair and celebrate the work they have done. The programme began in 2007 and has continued to grow over the years with moves to more classroom based inquiry projects that are known as *Mawkina'masultinej* (let's learn together) projects.

The programme has now spread from Nova Scotia to other provinces and territories, as an effective and engaging way for Indigenous and non-Indigenous students to understand and apply mathematical concepts and principles.

Dr. Lunney Borden has also begun a spin off outreach program known as Connecting math to Our Lives and Communities. The programme was designed for students in Grades 4 through 12 as a means to encourage youth to examine and investigate the value of mathematics in their lives and develop an appreciation for how mathematics can have power to shape their futures. Such learning supports students and encourages them to participate in further studies in mathematics and science and develop increased confidence in their mathematical abilities. It also provides opportunities for students to see that mathematics can be a powerful tool for helping the world.

This programme, now entering its third year, is run in four Mi'kmaw and three African Nova Scotian communities in Eastern Nova Scotia. The programme involved Bachelor of Education and undergraduate science and math students working with the school students every two weeks on issues of interest to them. Project work focused on *Reading and Writing the World with Mathematics*, through exploration of social justice issues such as water security and the environment, to patterns and logical reasoning, including technology and coding. Each year the programme ends with an on campus Math Camp day to celebrate the learning that has happened throughout the year and to once again invite students to learn mathematics with both university professors and community Elders.

Source: www.showmeyourmath.ca.

Using learning activities that reflect Indigenous practices or are popular among Indigenous students

A further promising practice that Canadian schools use to engage Indigenous students is to diversify learning activities to include those that draw on Indigenous history and culture or are popular with Indigenous students. These include culturally-based inquiry processes, outdoor and wilderness education programmes and using reservation ecosystems to teach science.

An example of land-based learning is found in Yukon, in the First Hunt, First Fish programme. The course content is established by the local Indigenous community and is popular among students. Schools have had some challenges related to meeting health and safety requirements, but they have largely been overcome.

The learning activities that schools use can make the curriculum much more relevant to Indigenous students' lives, for example by incorporating local places, history and events. These activities will also enrich learning for all students. A specific example of a tailored learning activity is the History in the Hills programme, where the classroom is taken to Indigenous archaeological sites and led by the teachings of First Nations and Métis peoples (Toulouse, 2013).

In one school we visited, Indigenous children were being mentored by a successful local entrepreneur. The students' recent achievements included publishing a bilingual children's book, releasing a language app and making a movie. They won awards for both the book and the app and donated their prize money to the local Head Start centre.

In Queensland, through a diverse range of in-school and extra-curricular activities, the Clontarf Foundation provides mentoring and coaching to Indigenous male students in secondary schools who are disengaged or at risk of disengaging. The Clontarf Foundation builds on Indigenous male students' passion for football to encourage behavioural change, including improving discipline, self-esteem, life skills and employment prospects. Fundamental to this is the development of values, skills and abilities that will assist students to achieve better life outcomes.

Providing a dedicated room for Indigenous students

Providing a dedicated room within schools for Indigenous students gives them a safe place to be and helps them feel they belong. It can provide a respite from the noise and intensity of some school environments, which can be difficult to cope with for children who have transitioned from on-reserve schools. A number of Indigenous students commented to us that these rooms provided them with a place to be away from the racism of other students.

In addition, such rooms provide a space where staff can provide support to students and students can support one another. We saw several examples of such rooms in the field visits, all of which were well utilised and valued by the Indigenous students we met in these schools.

In a high school in Alberta, the dedicated Indigenous students' room is used as part of a graduate coaching programme. Two coaches are available in the room to assist students. One is an academic coach and the other is an Indigenous co-ordinator, who assists students with issues that may be getting in the way of their study programme. Staff at the school have high expectations that students will graduate, and they hold students accountable for working hard to achieve this.

At one school we visited that did not have such a room, the students raised this with us as an improvement they would like to see. They said they would be happy to have somewhere to be that would be "their place".

We are aware that such rooms can be seen as a form of segregation, which can limit the extent of integration of Indigenous students with non-Indigenous students. We would argue, however, that students will only use these rooms if they see benefit in doing so. The use of such rooms is neither compulsory nor exclusive.

In some schools, non-Indigenous students also use these rooms. In some cases, they do so to be with their Indigenous friends, while in other cases it is because they do not feel safe in the wider school during break times. We also acknowledge that while the rooms provide respite for students, they do not address the underlying attitudes and behaviours that lead to students feeling uncomfortable or unsafe.

Providing learning opportunities in Indigenous languages

Offering one or more Indigenous languages to all students builds knowledge, skills and understanding of Indigenous peoples and cultures. Offering Indigenous languages also emphasises the importance and value of Indigenous languages to students, their families and school staff. For Indigenous students, this may be the only opportunity in their schooling years to learn their own language.

A reminder of the importance of language for young Indigenous people is found in the powerful lyrics of "Gentle Warrior":[6]

> I'm trying to speak but I can't find my words
> They snatched it away, shattered my world
>
> [...]
>
> I lost my talk, my courage, my pride
> For 500 years it's been hiding inside

Both teachers and Indigenous students we met expressed disappointment that, in most schools, Indigenous languages are only offered in certain grades and rarely, if ever, at senior levels of high school.

Varying assessment methods

Students' motivation, confidence and achievement can be encouraged through the use of a range of assessment techniques. Exams are necessarily narrow in perspective, so using a broad range of assessments can focus more on students' strengths and build a more enduring sense of efficacy and achievement. Examples include portfolios and performances.

Ensuring that all children and young people are acknowledged for what they know and can do and their interests and aspirations is important for student motivation. A Māori parent in New Zealand summed it up this way: "We should be focusing on success. We need to celebrate the kids' success in all areas, so that they can be proud achievers, passionate and have that confidence." (Meyer et al., 2010).

New Zealand's National Certificate of Education Achievement (NCEA) focuses on recognising, in senior secondary schools, what students know and can do, and where a much wider body of knowledge, including indigenous knowledge and skills, could be valued. Indigenous students have improved outcomes in achieving qualifications under this more flexible system. In addition, NCEA uses a range of assessment methodologies, allows very flexible collation of credits across a range of subject areas, and students can complete their qualification over more than one school year without necessarily having to complete lower level qualifications.[7]

Visibility of Indigenous people in leadership or governance roles within the school

Ensuring that there are Indigenous people in leadership and governance roles, as well as in other roles in the school, can instil a sense of belonging among Indigenous students. This point was raised by the older Indigenous students we met. One group stated that while they would like to have more Indigenous teachers at the school, having more teachers of colour would also help them to feel more comfortable at school.

There are a number of ways to actively recruit suitably skilled Indigenous people into the teaching profession. For example, teachers with language or cultural competence can be recruited and recognised through active selection and remuneration systems.

To support strong retention rates, Indigenous school leaders and teachers can be supported to remain in teaching through the use of mentors, networks and other support systems. In addition, school leaders may need to actively manage the workload of Indigenous teachers to prevent them being overburdened with the responsibilities of non-Indigenous teachers for Indigenous students. For example, Indigenous teachers may be asked to liaise with all Indigenous parents, rather than just the parents of students the Indigenous teacher teaches. Where workload pressures are not managed effectively, Indigenous teachers may not remain in teaching, and their experiences may make it more difficult to recruit further Indigenous teachers.

At the governance level, some school boards have designated Indigenous representation to ensure there is an Indigenous perspective at this level. An elementary school in Alberta increased the size of its Parent Council, to encourage greater involvement and input from Indigenous parents.

Involvement of Indigenous students' families with the school

Families that are positively engaged with their children's school are likely to encourage their children to attend school and engage constructively in school activities. Thus, creating inviting and welcoming environments for Indigenous families is important, as are active engagement policies that reach out to the community and provide opportunities for parents, other family members and the community to engage with the school, both on and off school grounds.

A school we visited in Alberta holds family nights throughout the year. Families meet with school staff over a meal at the school, and there is generally an Indigenous speaker. These are well attended and help to build a bridge between the school and students' families. Another school in Alberta also holds regular dinners for families and offers education programmes for parents in areas such as numeracy.

One principal we met provided an alarm clock to every child in the school. She commented that morning routines are not always well established, as parents in the community are often not in paid employment. The alarm clocks provided a way for her to talk to students and their families about the importance of punctuality, and also gave the students and their families a way to address this issue, which we understand it has done.

Roles for Elders within the school

The use of Elders in schools, as teachers, guides and mentors for students and teachers, is a further way to respect Indigenous peoples and their cultures and to provide opportunities for relevant learning for Indigenous students. In our field visits, we visited a number of schools that have Elders involved in teaching and guiding roles within schools and, in some cases, we were able to interview these Elders.

While there are clear benefits for students, relationships between schools and Elders also build staff capability and develop stronger links between the school and the local community.

Professional development for teachers and school leaders

To achieve classroom environments that honour Indigenous students' cultures, languages, world views and knowledge, teachers (most of whom are not Indigenous) need opportunities to develop their capabilities in relation to these areas. Having this capability development as an expectation and part of initial teacher education is essential, in addition to ongoing professional learning and development for teachers and school leaders.

In particular, teachers should have access to professional development opportunities to improve their knowledge and appreciation of the local community's historical, cultural and social context. Without this, they will struggle to provide localised, relevant curriculum for all of their students. The Northwest Territories addresses this through a three-day programme for new teachers, including one full day for an intensive awareness workshop on the history and legacy of residential schools.

Assessing how well teachers are prepared to teach Indigenous curriculum content can be done through teacher questionnaires. An example from Alberta is adding tailored questions on teacher preparedness in relation to Indigenous content to the Teaching and Learning International Survey, an international survey of teachers run by the OECD.

Providing Indigenous support workers within and/or across schools

Dedicated Indigenous advisory or support workers are a further means to provide support and guidance to students, teachers and school leaders. In the field visits, we saw two models of Indigenous support workers, one that involves working within a single school and the other that involves working across a number of schools.

Indigenous support workers within schools tend to monitor and support individual Indigenous students and their classroom teachers. They may have a particular focus on tracking and helping Indigenous students to attend and engage in school activities every day. They may also work directly with teachers on their teaching strategies and practices, and lead improvements in the curriculum and learning activities. They are often a connecting point with Indigenous parents and can lead whole-of-school activities to build cultural competencies.

Indigenous support workers who focus across schools interface more with school leadership than with individual students or teachers. Their role is often to incentivise and support school leaders to improve conditions for Indigenous students. This means, for example, helping school leaders to consciously track the engagement and progress of Indigenous students, and to identify and effectively address any barriers to learning that arise.

Both types of support workers intervene and advocate for individual students when there are high-stakes decisions, such as suspensions, and where they believe there is racist behaviour by teachers against Indigenous students. An example of the latter we were alerted to was an inspection of Indigenous students' school uniforms when they stepped off the bus from the local reserve when it arrived at the school. The inspections were apparently undertaken in full view of all students. Because of the efforts of an Indigenous support worker and two Indigenous staff at the school, this negative practice was stopped.

Re-engagement programmes for students who disengage or drop out of school

Truancy services can be used in a highly active and positive way to identify why students are disengaging from school and what is needed to get them back on track. Noticing early that students are not attending and taking action to resolve this and any underlying issues send a message to students that they are valued.

The establishment of an Individualised Learning Centre in Yukon is helping students who have disengaged or dropped out to continue with their studies. The Centre provides students with a range of programmes that will enable them to graduate. Learning is self-paced, and students receive individualised support from teachers and support workers.

An example of a re-engagement programme from Australia is the Big Picture programme, designed in the United States. The programme is designed for students who are at high risk of leaving school prior to completing Grade 12. The programme works with home-group classes of 12-15 students. Individual learning plans, prepared collaboratively with each of the students, their parents and teachers, are based on the student's personal interest and passions. Mentoring relationships are established to support all students on a regular basis. Students also undertake workplace internships (Doyle and Hill, 2008).

Notes

1. Headcount of students who have been withdrawn or permanently/removed from school.

2. (The act of) forcing someone, or being forced, to leave a school (Cambridge Dictionary).

3. The act of not allowing someone to go to school (Cambridge Dictionary).

4. A punishment in which a person is temporarily not allowed to go to school (Cambridge Dictionary).

5. For further information, see: www.australiancurriculum.edu.au/crosscurriculumpriorities/ aboriginal-and-torres-strait-islander-histories-and-cultures/overview

6. For a video and further information, see: https://nac-cna.ca/en/ritajoesong/gentle-warrior.

7. For further information, see: www.nzqa.govt.nz/qualifications-standards/qualifications/ ncea/understanding-ncea/how-ncea-works/.

References

Bishop, R. and M. Berryman (2010), "*Te Kotahitanga:* Culturally responsive professional development for teachers", *Teacher Development*, Vol. 14, Issue 2.

Christenson, S.L., A.L. Reschly and C. Wylie (eds.) (2012), *Handbook of Student Engagement*, Springer, New York, www.researchgate.net/publication/310773130 _Handbook_of_Student_Engagement.

Doyle, L. and R. Hill (2008), *Our Children, Our Future: Achieving Improved Primary and Secondary Education Outcomes for Indigenous Students: An overview of investment opportunities and approaches*, Social Ventures Australia, Sydney, http://socialventures.com.au/assets/Our_Children_Our_Future.pdf .

Dweck, C.S. (2006), *Mindset: The New Psychology of Success*, Random House, New York.

Hooper, S. et al. (1999), *School and family group conferences: Te Hui Whakatika* (a time for making amends), paper presented at the Keeping Young People in School Summit Conference on Truancy, Suspensions and Effective Alternatives, Auckland.

Meyer, L. et al. (2010), "Evaluation of *Te Kotahitanga*: 2004-2008", Report to the Ministry of Education, Ministry of Education, New Zealand, Wellington.

OECD (2016a), PISA 2015 Database, www.oecd.org/pisa/data/2015database/.

OECD (2016b), *Low-Performing Students: Why They Fall Behind and How to Help Them Succeed*, PISA, OECD Publishing, Paris, http://dx.doi.org/10.1787/9789264250 246-en.

OECD (2015), "What do parents look for in their child's school?", *PISA in Focus*, No. 51, OECD Publishing, Paris, http://dx.doi.org/10.1787/5js1qfw4n6wj-en.

OECD (2013a), *PISA 2012 Results: Ready to Learn (Volume III): Students' Engagement, Drive and Self-Beliefs*, PISA, OECD Publishing, Paris, http://dx.doi.org/10.1787/ 9789264201170-en.

Schunk, D.H. and F. Pajares (2009), "Self-efficacy theory", in K. R. Wentzel and A. Wigfield, *Handbook of Motivation at School*, Routledge, New York, pp. 35-53.

Show Me Your Math (2017), http://showmeyourmath.ca/.

Toulouse, P.R. (2013), *Beyond Shadows: First Nations, Métis and Inuit Student Success*, Canadian Teachers' Federation, Ottawa, www.ctf-fce.ca/Research-Library/Beyond Shadows_EN_Web.pdf.

Truth and Reconciliation Commission of Canada (2015), *Truth and Reconciliation Commission of Canada: Calls to Action*, Truth and Reconciliation Commission of Canada, Winnipeg, www.trc.ca/websites/trcinstitution/File/2015/Findings/Calls_ to_Action_English2.pdf.

Young, W. M. (2010), "An Investigation of exemplary teaching practices of teachers of Native American Students", Dissertation, University of Nevada, Las Vegas, http://digitalscholarship.unlv.edu/cgi/viewcontent.cgi?article=1900&context=thesesdis sertations.

Chapter 7

Supporting educational achievement among Indigenous students

Achievement is a multidimensional concept, which can relate to many aspects of life and vary according to an individual's aspirations. Educational systems can support achievement by providing students with the opportunities to develop the skills to realise their ambitions and participate fully in society. This is crucial for their well-being and for society as a whole. This chapter examines the importance of achievement for students, progress among jurisdictions in monitoring achievement and patterns in achievement. Six key levers have been identified to improve student achievement: high-quality early learning and teaching, leadership, extra support for students, engagement of families, and regular monitoring.

The statistical data for Israel are supplied by and under the responsibility of the relevant Israeli authorities. The use of such data by the OECD is without prejudice to the status of the Golan Heights, East Jerusalem and Israeli settlements in the West Bank under the terms of international law.

Achievement is a multifaceted concept. For many, if not most of us, life satisfaction, happiness, positive relationships with family and others, sound physical and mental health, secure employment and housing, a sense of belonging and contributing, and the pursuit of interests and aspirations are considered desirable outcomes. These are all indicators of well-being, but many are also achievements or the results of achievements. Not every child and young person will experience these in their lifetime.

Indigenous communities will each have their own priorities, aspirations and definitions of success, as will individuals and families within these communities. Speaking to teachers, parents and community members at a high school in Ottawa, Senator Murray Sinclair, Chair of the Truth and Reconciliation Commission of Canada, set out four questions that education systems should help all children to answer: "Where do I come from? Where am I going? Why am I here? Who am I?" (Anderson, 2016).

In New Zealand, Sir Mason Durie defined success as: "… where (Māori) can participate fully, as Māori, in *te ao Māori* (the Māori world) and *te ao whānaui* (wider society)" (Durie, 2006).

The role of education systems is to ensure that all children have the opportunity to develop the skills they need to realise their ambitions and to operate effectively in society. This chapter considers the extent to which the education systems in the jurisdictions participating in this study are delivering well for Indigenous students. It examines the importance of achievement for students, progress among jurisdictions in monitoring achievement, patterns in achievement, and policies and practices to improve student achievement.

Why achievement matters

Skilled individuals consistently have a range of better life outcomes than those with lower levels of skills. Highly skilled people are more likely to be good citizens, trust others, enjoy good health and have greater economic independence.

The OECD Survey of Adult Skills, a product of the Programme for the International Assessment of Adult Competencies, has found that having poor skills in literacy and numeracy limits people's access to better-paying and more rewarding jobs. By contrast, among the OECD countries that have had the largest expansion of university-level education over the past few decades, most still see rising earnings differentials for tertiary graduates. This suggests that the increase in the number of knowledge workers has not led to a decrease in their pay, as has been the case for low-skilled workers (OECD, 2013).

As the economic and social benefits for the highly skilled keep rising, the economic and social penalties for individuals without adequate skills are becoming more severe. Providing all individuals with the knowledge and skills to participate fully in our economies and societies, and to collaborate, compete and connect is essential for societal well-being, cohesion and economic growth.

A society where outcomes for individuals are determined primarily by their family circumstances, rather than their innate talents, is losing a great deal, both for society as a whole and for individuals who are thwarted from realising their ambitions. When such groups are growing demographically, as is the case for all three Indigenous populations in this study, these societies will undoubtedly face poorer economic prospects as well as greater risks to social cohesion.

Equity in education can be viewed through two dimensions: fairness and inclusion. Equity as fairness implies that personal or socio-economic circumstances, such as gender or family background, are not obstacles to success in education. Equity as inclusion means ensuring that all students reach at least a basic minimum level of skills. Equitable education systems are those that are both fair and inclusive, and support students to reach their learning potential (Schleicher, 2014).

In considering the extent to which an education system as a whole is equitable, findings from PISA 2015 show that 29.2% of students across OECD countries are resilient, meaning that they beat the socio-economic odds against them and exceed expectations compared to students in other countries. On this indicator of system performance, Canada performs better than either Australia or New Zealand in mitigating the socio-economic circumstances of disadvantaged students (Figure 7.1). Thus, the Canadian education system as a whole has strengths that should be able to deliver sound education experiences and outcomes to Canadian Indigenous students.

When considering inclusion in education, PISA 2015 demonstrates that approximately 23% of students in OECD countries did not reach the baseline level in mathematics. This is the level of mathematics proficiency considered necessary to function effectively in everyday life and most types of employment. It is very likely that students who lack basic skills at this age will either drop out of the education system and not finish upper secondary school or will continue studying but struggle to meet the requirements of school leaving qualifications, without considerable additional support. In both cases, students are unlikely to be well prepared for entering the workforce or for some aspects of everyday living, such as managing their financial affairs (Schleicher, 2014).

Progress in monitoring achievement

Data on student achievement is available from Alberta, Manitoba, Nova Scotia, New Zealand and Queensland. While comparisons based on assessments in different education systems are challenging, this study is more focused on understanding whether improvements are being achieved over time, the extent of any such improvements and what might lie behind them. As this study is intended to help participating jurisdictions to learn from one another, an emphasis on success and where improvements are occurring is more relevant than a comparative analysis across jurisdictions.

Most of the data in this section relates to 2010 and 2015, although Queensland did provide data for 2005. More complete data was provided by participating jurisdictions on mathematics than on other subjects, so much of the analysis has focused on mathematics.

Patterns in achievement

At lower secondary school in Alberta and Nova Scotia, just over one-third of Indigenous students and just over half of non-Indigenous students are proficient or highly proficient in mathematics. Students' proficiency levels in mathematics decline from lower secondary to upper secondary school for both Indigenous and non-Indigenous students. The size of the gap between the two groups of students is significant and remains constant (Figure 7.2).

Figure 7.1. Percentage of resilient students, 2015

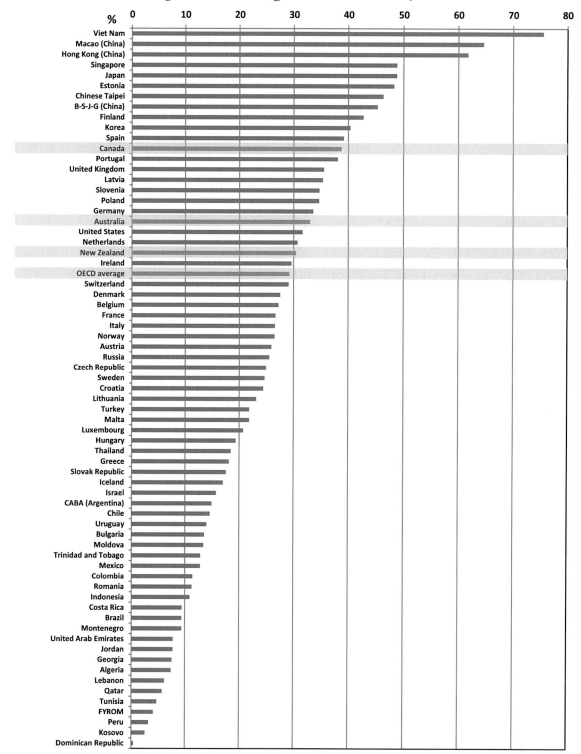

Note: A student is classified as resilient if he or she is in the bottom quarter of the PISA index of economic, social and cultural status (ESCS) in the country/economy of assessment and performs in the top quarter of students among all countries/economies, after accounting for socio-economic status.
Countries and economies are ranked in descending order of the percentage of resilient students.
Source: OECD (2016a), PISA 2015 Database, Table I.6.7, www.oecd.org/pisa/data/2015database/.
StatLink ⋙ http://dx.doi.org/10.1787/888933432786.

Figure 7.2. Middle-high and high level of proficiency in mathematics among Indigenous and non-Indigenous students in Canada, 2015

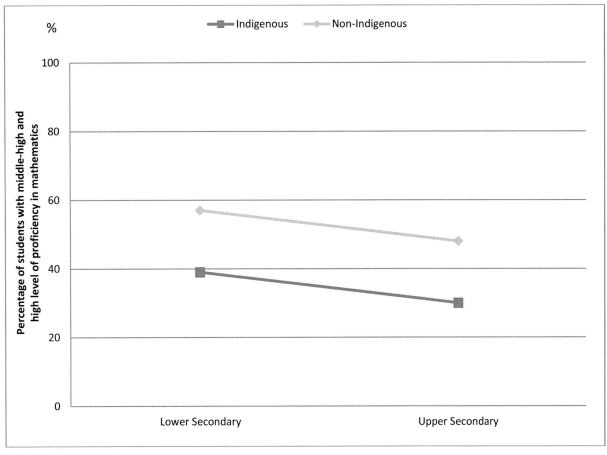

Notes: In the figure, Canadian data include only Alberta and Nova Scotia. In Alberta, middle-high level means that the score achieved was in the upper 50% of students within the "acceptable category", and high level means that the score achieved was in the "excellent" category. In Nova Scotia, middle-high level means that the score achieved was as expected at the end of the course, and high level means that the score achieved was significantly above the minimum expectation at the end of the course.

Sources: Alberta Education and Nova Scotia Education (2016), Data Questionnaires.

Monitoring of Indigenous students' achievement tends to be more effective in the earlier years of schooling than in later years. Monitoring student progress in the early years enables system leaders to notice changes (both positive and negative) and to respond accordingly. It also enables a system-wide view of whether strategies, policies and resourcing decisions are having the intended impact.

Alberta, Manitoba, New Zealand and Queensland were all able to provide data on graduation rates for Indigenous students. While there are variations in the exact requirements for graduation in each jurisdiction, they all involve the accumulation of credits and/or some other forms of demonstrated proficiency across a mix of subjects. However, the definition used for Figures 7.3 and 7.4 are students graduating from a high school (upper) secondary, ISCED Level 3 programme.

Just over half of Indigenous students in Canada graduate from high school, or/within the typical high school timeframe, while this is largely the norm for non-Indigenous students (Figure 7.3). Across both groups of students, girls are more likely to graduate than boys.

This result indicates severe inequity within the education system for Indigenous students, both a lack of fairness and a high level of exclusion. Such poor outcomes cannot be accepted for any group within an education system. The life outcomes for the Indigenous young people negatively affected by these results will be significantly curtailed. All children have the right to expect access to a sound education system that will support them to succeed. This is the very reason why the eight jurisdictions participating in this study are doing so.

Figure 7.3. Graduation rates of Indigenous students by gender in Canada, 2015

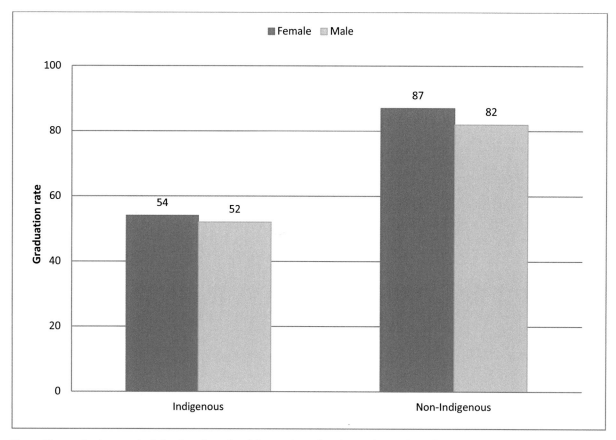

Notes: The graduation rate is defined as the ratio of the number of students who graduate from a high school/(upper) secondary programme / ISCED Level 3 programme during the reference year to the number of new entrants in this programme. In the figure, Canadian data include only Alberta and Manitoba.

Sources: Alberta Education and Manitoba Education (2016), Data Questionnaires.

Graduation rates for Indigenous students have been increasing over time in all jurisdictions in this study. In particular, Alberta, Manitoba and Queensland show striking improvements between 2010 and 2015 (Figure 7.4).

Figure 7.4. Graduation rates of Indigenous students in Queensland, New Zealand and Canada, 2005, 2010 and 2015

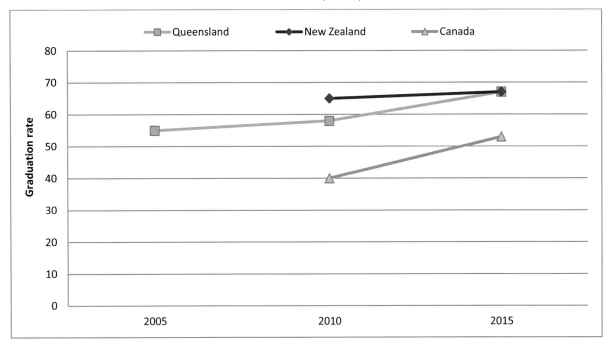

Notes: The graduation rate is defined as the ratio of the number of students who graduate from a high school/(upper) secondary programme / ISCED Level 3 programme during the reference year to the number of new entrants in this programme. In the figure, Canadian data include only Alberta and Manitoba.

Sources: Alberta Education, Manitoba Education, Queensland Department of Education and Training and New Zealand Ministry of Education (2016), Data Questionnaires.

Policies and practices to improve achievement

At the system level, there are six key levers to improve the experiences and outcomes of disadvantaged students:

- high quality early learning, through working with families and the provision of tailored early childhood education

- leadership in schools that is actively focused on student outcomes, responsive to student needs and resourceful in putting in place the necessary educational provision

- high-quality teaching, including high expectations for all students, respectful relationships with students and relevant and responsive curriculum delivery

- provision of tailored support in needed areas, in addition to (not instead of) regular classroom instruction

- enlisting the active involvement of families in helping their children to learn

- regular monitoring of each child's progress and timely actions in response to this information.

While programmes to lift student achievement can be helpful as an impetus for change, there are unlikely to be sustained positive benefits where these are led by people external to the school, are time limited and do not improve the leadership and teaching capability at the school. Unless there is vigilance within the school on what is happening for each child and effective responses are put in place, where appropriate, the status quo will re-emerge and system-wide change will not be achieved.

Programmes can, however, be the interruption that is needed to change mindsets and lift pedagogical competence. As one principal in a language programme in Queensland noted: "... the pedagogical reality is that socio-economic and language barriers can be overcome – the programme has helped staff see this. It has raised their expectations of what the kids can do." (ACER, 2013).

Like schools that are achieving improvements in student engagement, schools that are making progress on student achievement among Indigenous students are using most, if not all, of the levers listed above. Thus, it is the combined effort over a sustained period that matters for improvements.

A study of successful programmes in schools in Canadian Indigenous communities in a range of locations found that despite the rich diversity in approaches and circumstances, a number of common characteristics distinguished these schools, in varying degrees of intensity. The study concluded that the elements of their success were rooted in strong leadership and governance structures, often with long tenure, multiple programmes and supports for learners, exceptional language and cultural programmes, and secure and welcoming climates for children and families (Fulford et al., 2007).

In some cases, schools are assisted by their education ministries and are making good use of the policies and resources provided by them. In other cases, schools are accessing what they need themselves, often in partnership with Indigenous communities. There is much that education ministries can do to support schools to deliver better learning opportunities for Indigenous students. While there are clearly examples of schools that are delivering sound education for Indigenous students, improvements across the system as a whole cannot rely on individual principals and teachers to deliver such improvements. Guidance and support must be provided to accelerate change.

Early learning

To ensure Indigenous children start school on the same footing as other children, high-quality, tailored and responsive early childhood education and care must be provided to every child from at least two years of age. Early interventions of this nature can ensure that children develop the language skills and emotional stability needed to develop well and to be ready for school (Box 7.1). As a researcher from Manitoba commented: "Starting behind means staying behind."

To be effective, these programmes are generally based close to where the children and their families live. The Families as First Teachers programme was developed in Queensland in 2005 to support Indigenous parents, where their children were not attending established preschool programmes (Brim and Mannion, 2012). It was implemented in 2009 in the Northern Territory. Since 2012, the programme has delivered the Abecedarian Approach Australia (3A) programme, which combines literacy and parenting approaches, across 21 very remote sites, with a further 14 very remote sites serviced by a mobile team across the Northern Territory. It is intended to engage the whole family, to operate from a strength-based approach, to be culturally responsive, and to involve intergenerational learning (Dreise and Perrett, forthcoming).

Box 7.1. Strong early development and learning in Manitoba

A tailored early childhood education and care centre was established in a predominantly Indigenous neighbourhood in Winnipeg in 2012 to address poor levels of early development and learning identified at school entry. The centre is based on the Abecedarian Approach and includes a research evaluation comparing children in the programme with a control group. Approximately 80% of children at the centre are Indigenous. Each child is tracked in terms of his/her development, and they will continue to be tracked into their schooling years.

The impact on children's language development from their first year in the programme is more than double the control group, as shown below, comparing average percentage changes in language scores for both groups.

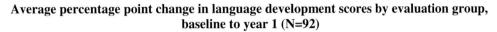

Average percentage point change in language development scores by evaluation group, baseline to year 1 (N=92)

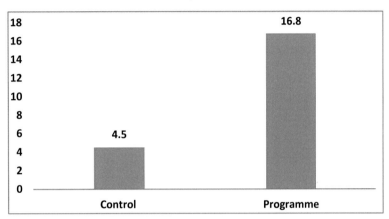

Notes: Analysis of Variance/Covariance controls for baseline Language Development score, age and gender of child.
Language development score differences between the Programme and Control groups are statistically significant at the 0.02 level.
Source: Healthy Child Manitoba Office, 2017.

Children enter the centre at three months of age and attend five days a week, full-time, until they start school. Each child has a primary caregiver at the centre, whose role is to provide individualised, relationship-based care. The focus is on language development, which supports greater subsequent cognitive and social and emotional development. The language-oriented Abecedarian Approach has three main pillars:

- Enriched caregiving
- Conversational reading
- LearningGames®.

Engagement with children's families is also an important part of the programme, both to support parents in enhancing their children's development and learning and to address any barriers or issues that families may be facing. Engagement with families is strength-based and occurs through regular home visits, involving parents in the centre, a monthly parent support group and a co-located drop-in resource centre.

Recognition of Indigenous cultures is also a key aspect of the programme. An Indigenous Programme Co-ordinator is on-staff, and Indigenous art, knowledge and cultural practices are woven into the operation of the centre.

Staff are drawn from the local community, including Indigenous staff, which helps to strengthen the connections with families and the community and keeps staff turnover relatively low. All new staff are provided with comprehensive training.

Source: D'Souza, M. (2016), *The Abecedarian Approach in Manitoba's Early Childhood Community*, Research Faculty, School of Health Sciences and Community Services Red River College, Winnipeg, Manitoba, www.oise.utoronto.ca/atkinson/UserFiles/File/Events /20160602_SI2016/SI2016_Presentations/The_Abecedarian_Approach_in_a_North_Winnipeg_Community_-_Melanie_DSouza.pdf.

Another early learning programme with positive results for Indigenous children is the One World Child Development Centre in Calgary (Alberta). One World describes itself as a two-generation preschool programme designed to provide comprehensive, integrated early intervention to simultaneously address the needs of preschool children and their parents/caregivers. Of the 50 children enrolled at One World each year, approximately 36% are of Indigenous heritage (Benzies et al., 2011).

Leadership

A model of system-level leadership is that of Enhanced Education Agreements. In an example we saw in New Brunswick, the agreement had been signed by the Chief and the Education Superintendent. The agreement reflects a partnership between the First Nation community, the provincial education system and the school. Clear goals are set, and a plan of action is established to deliver on these goals. In the school we visited, these goals were to create a strong nurturing and cultural environment for the First Nations children who attend the school and to ensure that educational equity is achieved for these students.

In every school we visited as part of this study where there were whole-of-school sustained improvements for Indigenous students, we found that the principal was an active and effective leader. These leaders were clear about their fundamental goals. They had achieved alignment on these goals and the actions needed to realise them across teachers, students, parents and the wider community the school serves. These leaders have high expectations of students and teachers and use every possible means to provide positive and effective learning environments for all students. They focus on learning and achievement (Dreise and Perrett, forthcoming).

A principal from New Brunswick emphasised to us the role and responsibility of principals in ensuring that Indigenous students achieve: "It's our responsibility to find the resources we need ... these are children, who want to learn"(Box 7.2).

The Best Evidence Synthesis (Robinson, Hohepa and Lloyd, 2009) investigated the types and dimensions of leadership that are most strongly associated with better student achievement. The findings argue for a shift in leadership issues away from teachers to focus on what and how teachers are teaching, and what and how children and young people are learning and achieving. This is pedagogical leadership: what happens at the interactional and relationship levels to make a difference in educational outcomes. An inclusive style of pedagogical leadership embraces all who are able to make a difference in student outcomes.

In the field visits, we met a number of very effective school leaders who are consciously improving the education experiences and outcomes of Indigenous students. They were smart, deep thinkers, superb communicators and, in the main, humble. These leaders, and others like them, are a critical resource jurisdictions can tap into to provide guidance and support to other school leaders who are struggling to achieve progress. These leaders could also provide advice on system-wide initiatives, in terms of how they are likely to impact on the ground.

Box 7.2. A high-performing elementary school in New Brunswick

An elementary school in New Brunswick has almost eliminated academic and behavioural gaps between Indigenous students and non-Indigenous students, achieving high results overall. The school is based in a low socio-economic area and has a significant Indigenous student population from the nearby First Nation. The principal, staff, parents and students attribute the success of the school to the following:

- An Education Enhancement Agreement between the chief of the local First Nation and the Education Superintendent of the Ministry of Education. The agreement sets out joint objectives in providing high-quality education for students who reside on reserve and the roles and responsibilities of each party in achieving this.

- Early childhood education provision, based in the First Nation, which almost all children attend. The principal believes the introduction of this centre has been the most significant factor in improving the educational progress of the children.

- Each child's transition to school is carefully managed. Staff meet parents before children start school to learn about their child's interests, development and needs. Children and their parents visit the school before the year starts, and a welcome ceremony for children and their families takes place once the year has commenced.

- The principal and school staff are regular visitors to the First Nation, to continue to build relationships with the chief, parents and other community members. All teacher/parent discussions for children from the First Nation are held in the First Nation community. If there are disciplinary or other issues to resolve, the principal and/or staff will also seek to resolve these in the First Nation.

- The school has an Indigenous support worker, who liaises between each Indigenous child's parents and the school. The support worker checks that each Indigenous child is at school every day, puts strategies in place for children who face challenges in getting to school and works alongside other agencies to quickly address issues that may be negatively impacting on the child's ability to engage in school.

- The school provides a dedicated Indigenous students' room. It is a quiet, comfortable space for Indigenous children to be with other Indigenous children before school and at break times, and with the Indigenous support worker and teachers. Parents are also able to drop in, as are non-Indigenous children who want respite from regular school life or who simply want to be with their Indigenous school friends. The Indigenous students at this school described their room as their home base.

- The school uses a variety of learning activities to engage all children. One is Show Me Your Math (Box 6.1), which makes use of traditional Indigenous symbols, such as dreamcatchers, as a basis for understanding mathematical concepts. Another is the involvement of a local Indigenous entrepreneur, who works with the children on innovation projects such as a bilingual language app, for which they won an innovation award.

- Each child at this school is assessed regularly across a range of indicators. The principal and staff regularly review the progress and development of each child to ensure that steps are taken in a timely manner if any child is not progressing well.

Source: Field visits in New Brunswick, 2016.

High-quality teaching

A review of the international evidence on learning presents a set of guiding principles on the way education is planned and offered in classrooms, with a particular focus on equity (Dumont, Istance and Benavides, 2010):

- Learner centred: The learning environment needs to be focused on learning as the principal activity, not as an alternative to the critical role of teachers and other learning professionals, but dependent on them.

- Structured and well-designed: To be learner-centred requires careful design and high levels of professionalism. This still leaves room for inquiry and autonomous learning.

- Personalised: The learning environment is sensitive to individual and group differences in background, prior knowledge, motivation and abilities, and offers tailored and detailed feedback.

- Inclusive: The learning environment takes into consideration individual and group differences, including the struggling learners, and defines an education agenda that excludes no one.

- Social: Learning is effective when it takes place in group settings, when learners collaborate as an explicit part of the learning environment, and when there is a connection to community.

For disadvantaged students, high expectations of achievement by educators can make a huge difference. As Young (2010) explains: "By setting high expectations and building the trust necessary to reach those standards, teachers can offer students the possibility of success."

Having high expectations also relates to the types of teaching and learning strategies that teachers use with Indigenous students. For example, reliance on simple memorisation techniques in mathematics rather than conceptual learning means students will be less able to tackle more complex mathematics problems, and this may limit their future prospects in relation to mathematics (OECD, 2016b). Memorisation is quite common in New Zealand and Australia, where 35% of students in both countries report they learn mathematics primarily through memorisation. Just over a quarter of Canadian students (26%) report that they rely on memorisation rather than other techniques (above the OECD average of 21%).

Having high expectations of teachers is also important, as is professional development to assist them to provide more effective teaching and learning for students. Professional development and learning have greatest impacts when they are linked to a whole-of-school improvement plan and/or to specific achievement objectives for students (Timperley, 2008). Professional development can help teachers to understand school and student-level data, devise changes in teaching approaches and assess the impact of such changes in practice on student outcomes.

An example from New Zealand where progress for students has been achieved is the Learning and Change Networks (LCN). Schools voluntarily work together to boost student achievement in particular areas. This involves teachers from different schools interrogating their own and other schools' data, classroom observations across schools, involvement of students' views on their learning and persistence over some years. The success of these networks has been complemented by a New Zealand-wide initiative, Communities of Learning, to incentivise and assist all schools to work together for the benefit of their students. Another model called Māori Achievement Collaboratives (MACs) also existed alongside the LCN example. MACs were an adaptation of LCNs, tailored and targeted to build networks of school leaders focused on better outcomes for Māori learners and were strongly supported by the New Zealand Principals Federation. MACs also continued to operate in the *Kāhui Ako* environment.

Teachers may also benefit from professional development that helps them to better understand their students, their students' families and communities, the history of Indigenous peoples in their area and the cultural and historical significance of events, places and landmarks in the vicinity of the school community.

Both Australia and New Zealand set requirements for teachers' cultural competence. The Australian Professional Standards for Teachers specify what teachers should know and be able to do in order to teach Aboriginal and Torres Strait Islander students and to teach all Australian students about Aboriginal and Torres Strait Island culture and history. The requirements within the Standards are in two Focus Areas: 1.4) Strategies for teaching Aboriginal and Torres Strait Islander Students; and 2.4) Understand and respect Aboriginal and Torres Strait Islander people to promote reconciliation between Indigenous and non-Indigenous Australians.

It is critical that initial teacher education programmes prepare teachers well for the range of students they must teach. Thus, incorporating an evidence-based approach to teaching effectiveness for Indigenous students must be an integral part of every initial teacher education programme.

In the 2013 OECD Teaching and Learning International Survey, 12.7% of teachers reported a high need for professional development for teaching in a multicultural or multilingual setting. In Alberta, 3.8% of teachers reported a high need for such development, as did 4.4% of teachers in Australia (OECD, 2014).[1]

Extra support for students

Extra assistance and coaching for students can be helpful. Such support is most effective, however, when it is in addition to, rather than instead of, regular classroom instruction. At one school we visited, senior Indigenous students were enlisted (and compensated) to tutor younger Indigenous students. This school also runs a mentoring programme to provide Indigenous students with general support in their first year or two at the school.

One principal we spoke to emphasised the importance of ensuring that the most effective teachers are used to work with students who are struggling. He noted that, in his experience, extra support is sometimes provided by the least qualified or able teachers, while the most effective teachers continue to work with students who are progressing well.

An example of effective extra support is intensive language development for students whose first language or dialect is different from the language of instruction. Such support is necessary for these children to succeed in the schooling system. In Australia, Indigenous students, particularly in remote communities, are not always able to speak Standard Australian English (SAE). As these students speak some English, non-Indigenous teachers had interpreted this as meaning the students were proficient in SAE. However, once teachers had been trained in accurate language assessment and language teaching, students were able to rapidly improve in both their language proficiency and their performance in school.

The support of families

Helping families to actively support their children's learning can be effective in accelerating student learning. An example is an Australian project on literacy for Indigenous students. Parents were actively involved through parent workshops on literacy, guidance on reading activities they could undertake with their children, and communication and feedback between the school and students' families. Over a two-year period, students in this programme made gains of up to one year in their literacy levels. This improved achievement had positive flow-on effects to students' enrolment and attendance rates (Graham and Berman, 2013).

The Mutukaroa project was developed in a school in a disadvantaged neighbourhood in Auckland, New Zealand. Children are assessed when they start school, and these results are shared with parents. Parents are asked to undertake learning activities with their child every day. After six months, the child's assessment results are again shared with parents. Most parents are surprised by how much progress their child has made (the school provides exceptionally high standards of teaching and learning), and parents are asked to undertake a new set of activities with their child. As the cycle continues, parents build confidence and pride in their child's ability to learn and start to invest more time in interacting with both their child and the school. Once the parents and school are aligned, children's learning time is effectively doubled or more, and their learning accelerates.

Regular monitoring of each child

The effective schools we visited in this study all undertake early and ongoing assessment of individual student needs and progress. They actively use this information to tailor their education responses to individual students' needs.

An example in Australia that supports teachers to adopt such an approach is the Starting Block Programme, funded by the Cathy Freeman Foundation (Cathy Freeman is an Indigenous Australian Olympic gold medallist, who famously ran her victory lap at the Sydney Olympics draped in the Aboriginal flag). The Starting Block equips teachers with resources to measure and record student progress and achievement in literacy, attendance and general conduct on a daily basis. At the end of each term, students' families and community members attend Starting Block Awards ceremonies to recognise their achievements. The programme is designed to help children learn to set and realise personal goals.

Note

1. New Zealand did not participate in TALIS 2013.

References

Anderson, S. (2016), "Murray Sinclair: Education is key to reconciliation", rabble.ca blogs, Toronto, http://rabble.ca/blogs/bloggers/kairos-canada/2016/06/murray-sinclair-education-key-to-reconciliation.

ACER (Australian Council for Educational Research) (2013), *Evaluation of the Closing the Gap: Expansion of Intensive Literacy and Numeracy Programs for Indigenous Students program*, unpublished report to the Department of Education, Employment and Workplace Relations, ACER, Camberwell.

Benzies, K. et al. (2011), "Aboriginal Children and Their Caregivers Living with Low Income: Outcomes from a Two-Generation Preschool Program", *Journal of Child and Family Studies*, pp. 311-318, http://link.springer.com/article/10.1007%2Fs10826-010-9394-3.

Brim, R. and K. Mannion (2012), "Families as first teachers: Giving indigenous children a strong start for a brighter future", *Educating Young Children: Learning and Teaching in the Early Childhood Years*, Vol. 18, No. 2, pp. 8-12. http://search.informit.com.au/documentSummary;dn=681956357283872;res=IELHSS

D'Souza M (2016), *The Abecedarian Approach in Manitoba's Early Childhood Community*, Research Faculty, School of Health Sciences and Community Services Red River College, Winnipeg, Manitoba, www.oise.utoronto.ca/atkinson/UserFiles/File/Events/20160602_SI2016/SI2016_Presentations/The_Abecedarian_Approach_in_a_North_Winnipeg_Community_-_Melanie_DSouza.pdf.

Dumont, H., D. Istance and F. Benavides (eds.) (2010), *The Nature of Learning: Using Research to Inspire Practice*, OECD Publishing, Paris, http://dx.doi.org/10.1787/9789264086487-en.

Durie, M. (2006), *Measuring Māori Wellbeing*, New Zealand Treasury Guest Lecture Series, Wellington.

Dreise, T. and W. Perrett (forthcoming), "Promising Practices in Closing The Gap in Indigenous Education: A Literature Review Report for the OECD", OECD Publishing, Paris.

Fulford, G. et al. (2007), *Sharing our success: more case studies in Aboriginal schooling*, Society for the Advancement of Excellence in Education, Kelowna, www.academia.edu/3481931/Sharing_our_success_More_case_studies_in_Aboriginal_schooling.

Graham, L. and J. Berman (2013), *Final Project Evaluation: Closing the Gap* in NSW Independent Schools, NSW Association of Independent Schools, Sydney.

OECD (2016a), PISA 2015 Database, www.oecd.org/pisa/data/2015database/.

OECD (2016b), "Is memorisation a good strategy for learning mathematics?", *PISA in Focus*, No. 61, OECD Publishing, Paris, http://dx.doi.org/10.1787/5jm29kw38mlq-en.

OECD (2014), *TALIS 2013 Results: An International Perspective on Teaching and Learning*, TALIS, OECD Publishing, Paris, http://dx.doi.org/10.1787/97892 64196261-en.

OECD (2013), *OECD Skills Outlook 2013: First Results from the Survey of Adult Skills*, OECD Publishing, Paris, http://dx.doi.org/10.1787/9789264204256-en .

Robinson, V., M. Hohepa and C. Lloyd (2009), *School Leadership and Student Outcomes: Identifying What Works and Why*, New Zealand Ministry of Education, Wellington, www.educationcounts.govt.nz/publications/series/2515/60169/60170.

Schleicher, A. (2014), *Equity, Excellence and Inclusiveness in Education: Policy Lessons from Around the World*, International Summit on the Teaching Profession, OECD Publishing, Paris, http://dx.doi.org/10.1787/9789264214033-en.

Timperley, H. (2008), "Teacher professional learning and development", Educational Practices Series-18, International Academy of Education, Brussels.

Young, W. M. (2010), "An Investigation of exemplary teaching practices of teachers of Native American Students", Dissertation, University of Nevada, Las Vegas, http://digitalscholarship.unlv.edu/cgi/viewcontent.cgi?article=1900&context=thesesdis sertations.

Annex A

Overview of the education systems
in Canada, Australia and New Zealand

Canada

Responsibility for education

- In Canada, the 13 provinces and territories are responsible for education. The federal government is responsible for the education of First Nation students who attend on-reserve schools.

- Each jurisdiction has one or two ministries or departments which are responsible for organisation, delivery and assessment of the education system, from primary to post-secondary education. These responsibilities include the operation and administration of schools, curriculum development and implementation, personnel management and student enrolment.

- Provincial or territorial governments can delegate their authority to school boards or school districts. Schools often have responsibility for organisation of instruction (e.g. student careers, instruction time, choice of textbooks, grouping of students, teaching methods and day-to-day student assessment).

- Ministers of education and advanced education also set pan-Canadian educational priorities under the Council of Ministers of Education, Canada (CMEC).

Types of schools

- In Canada, schools serving Indigenous students can be located on reserve or off reserve.

- On-reserve schools are located inside designated reserves for First Nation people, and they are only composed of First Nation students. In 2010, among the 109 000 Indigenous students living on reserves, over 64% attended 515 schools on reserve, while 36% attended schools off reserve.

- Off-reserve schools serve both Indigenous and non-Indigenous students. In Canada's ten provinces and three territories, students have a choice between two types of off-reserve schools: public schools and private schools. In 2013/14, there were a total of 5 034 378 students enrolled in off-reserve elementary and secondary schools. At secondary level, in 2013, 93% of students were enrolled in public schools and 7% in private schools.

Budget for education

- Public funding for schools on reserve comes from the federal government.

- Off-reserve public schools are funded by the province or territory, but for private schools, the share of public funding varies from jurisdiction to jurisdiction. Private schools can be fully funded, partially funded or receive no public funding.

- Public funding for off-reserve schools is delivered either directly from the provincial or territorial government or through a mix of provincial transfers and local taxes. The federal government provides a small amount of financial support for post-secondary education and programmes that support skills development.

- Overall in 2014, Canada spent USD 12 967 per student each year from primary through tertiary education (above the OECD average of USD 10 493).

Education system

- As shown in Figure A.1, Canadian students begin compulsory education at age 6 and finish around the age of 16-18. In most OECD countries, compulsory education is from age 6 to age 16 or 17.

- In Canada, early childhood education and care (ECEC) is from age 3 to age 4, before kindergarten, which covers age 4 to age 5. With the exception of the last year prior to entering Grade 1, ECEC is mostly private, and access to it varies across jurisdictions.

Figure A.1. Overview of the education system in Canada

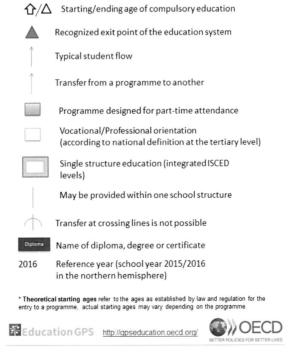

Source: OECD (2016), "Overview of the education system in Canada", OECD Education GPS, http://gpseducation.oecd.org/Content/MapOfEducationSystem/CAN/CAN_2011_EN.pdf.

References

OECD (2016), "Canada: Overview of the education system", OECD Education GPS, http://gpseducation.oecd.org/CountryProfile?primaryCountry=CAN&treshold=10&topic=EO.

OECD (2015), *Education Policy Outlook: Canada*, OECD Publishing, Paris, www.oecd.org/edu/EDUCATION%20POLICY%20OUTLOOK%20CANADA.pdf.

CMEC (Council of Ministers of Education Canada), "Education in Canada: An Overview", CMEC, Toronto, www.cmec.ca/299/Education-in-Canada-An-Overview/index.html.

AFN (Assembly of First Nations) (2012), "A Portrait of First Nations and Education", AFN, Ottawa, www.afn.ca/uploads/files/1_-_fact_sheet_-_a_portrait_of_first_nations_and_education.pdf.

Statistics Canada (2016), "Back to school…by the numbers", Statistics Canada, Ottawa, www.statcan.gc.ca/eng/dai/smr08/2016/smr08_210_2016.

The World Bank (2013), "Percentage of enrolment in secondary education in private institutions (%) from UNESCO Institute for Statistics", The World Bank, Washington, http://data.worldbank.org/indicator/SE.SEC.PRIV.ZS?locations=CA.

Australia

Responsibility for education

- In Australia, both state and territory governments and the Australian Government have responsibilities in education.

- State and territory governments are responsible for the delivery and funding of school and vocational education. They make most planning, structure and resource decisions, including personnel management. State and territory governments are also responsible for legislation relating to the establishment and accreditation of higher education courses.

- The Australian Government has special responsibilities in education and training for Indigenous students and migrants. It is also in charge of developing international partnerships in education. The Australian Government provides funding for schools, higher education institutions and vocational education and training.

- National and state or territory governments define education goals through intergovernmental arrangements.

Types of schools

- Australia has two types of schools: government schools and non-government schools (which include Catholic and independent schools). In 2016, 65.4% of students attended government schools, while 20.2% attended Catholic schools, and 14.4% were in independent schools.

Budget for education

- Government schools receive public funding. The majority of their funding comes from state and territory governments (91% of the total amount in 2013), while the Australian Government provides supplementary funding (9% in 2013).

- Non-government schools can receive public and private funding. While, the share between the two sources varies depending on jurisdictions, on average, public funding represents 57% of total non-government schools' income. The majority of the public funding comes from the Australian Government (72% of the total amount in 2013), while state and territory governments provide supplementary funding (28% in 2013).

- Private funding is provided by fees and charges, as well as private donations and income.

- In 2014, Australia spent USD 11 169 per student each year from primary through tertiary education, (compared to the OECD average of USD 10 493).

Education system

- As shown in Figure A.2, Australian students begin compulsory education at the age of 6 and finish around the age of 15. In most OECD countries, compulsory education is slightly longer, starting at age 6 and finishing at age 16 or 17.

- In Australia, early childhood education is not compulsory. It is delivered through a range of settings, including childcare centres and preschools (called kindergartens in some parts of Australia) in the year before full-time schooling. In 2015, the share of children in formal early childhood education and care was 16% at 0-1 years, 58% at 2-3 years and 93% at 4-5 years (excluding those already in school at this age) (Baxter, 2015).

Figure A.2. Overview of the education system in Australia

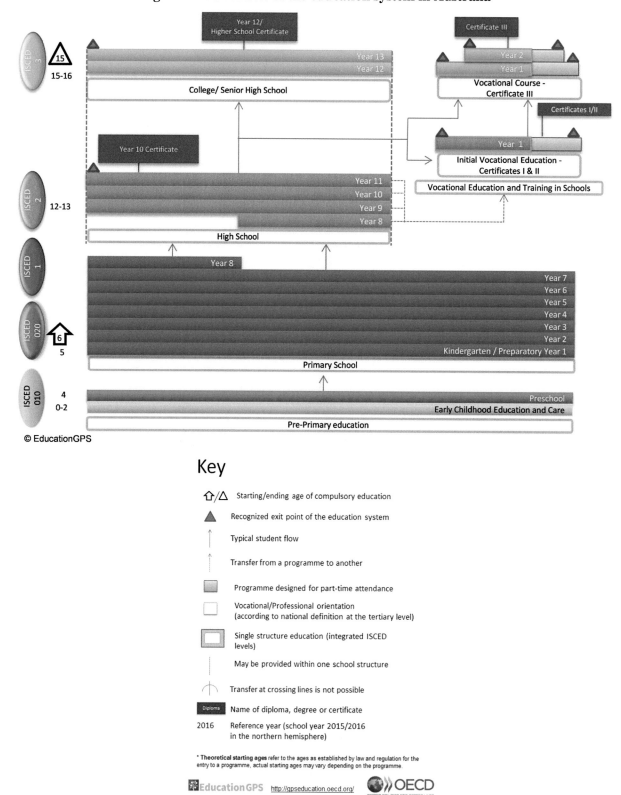

Source: OECD (2016), "Overview of the education system in Australia", OECD Education GPS, http://gpseducation.oecd.org/Content/MapOfEducationSystem/AUS/AUS_2011_EN.pdf.

References

Australian Qualifications Framework Council (2013), "Australian Qualifications Framework", Australian Qualifications Framework Council, Canberra, https://www.aqf.edu.au/sites/aqf/files/aqf-2nd-edition-january-2013.pdf.

Baxter, J. (2015), "Child care and early childhood education in Australia (Facts Sheet 2015)", Australian Institute of Family Studies, Melbourne, https://aifs.gov.au/sites/default/files/publication-documents/fs2015.pdf.

OECD (2016), Australia: Overview of the education system, OECD Education GPS, http://gpseducation.oecd.org/CountryProfile?primaryCountry=AUS&treshold=10&topic=EO.

OECD (2013), *Education Policy Outlook: Australia*, OECD Publishing, Paris, www.oecd.org/education/EDUCATION%20POLICY%20OUTLOOK%20AUSTRALIA_EN.pdf.

Department of Education and Training, "Funding for schools", Department of Education and Training, Canberra, www.education.gov.au/funding-schools.

Harrington, M. (2011), "Australian Government funding for schools explained", Parliamentary Library, Parliament of Australia, Canberra, www.aph.gov.au/binaries/library/pubs/bn/sp/schoolsfunding.pdf.

MCEETYA (Ministerial Council on Education, Employment, Training and Youth Affairs) (2008), "2008 National Report on Schooling in Australia", MCEETYA, http://scseec.edu.au/site/DefaultSite/filesystem/documents/Reports%20and%20publications/Archive%20Publications/National%20Report/ANR%202008.pdf.

New Zealand

Responsibility for education

- In New Zealand, the central government is responsible for education. The government sets education policy, and the Ministry of Education develops and implements it. The Ministry is in charge of curriculum and assessment standards for students and teachers. It provides funding and collaborates on cross-government actions.

- In practice, the government devolves most of management responsibilities to schools. Boards of Trustees, which govern each school, are accountable to the central government and the community. They ensure respect of the National Education Guidelines, decide on the school's education policies and manage staff and finances.

Types of schools

- Schools can be state schools (including regular state schools, Māori medium schools, special schools, and designated character schools), state-integrated schools (having a special character by being run by a particular religious faith or using specialist education methods) or independent schools. The majority of students (85%) attend state schools, with 10% enrolled in state-integrated schools and the remaining 5% in independent schools.

Budget for education

- State schools and state-integrated schools are mainly funded by the central government, through general taxation. They also receive supplementary funding, with voluntary donations from parents.

- Independent schools are funded by private sources through fees, and they receive some subsidy funding from the government, set each year by the Ministry of Education.

- In 2014, New Zealand spent USD 10 045 per student each year from primary through tertiary education (compared to the OECD average of USD 10 493).

Education system

- As shown in Figure A.3, students in New Zealand begin compulsory education at age 5 and finish at around age 16. In most OECD countries, compulsory education is from age 6 to age 16 or 17.

- In New Zealand, early childhood education and care starts at birth and continues to school entry age. Although participation is voluntary, attendance levels are high. In 2014, 87% of 3-year-olds were enrolled in ECEC, and 92% of 4-year-olds (one year before the beginning of compulsory education).

Figure A.3. Overview of the education system in New Zealand

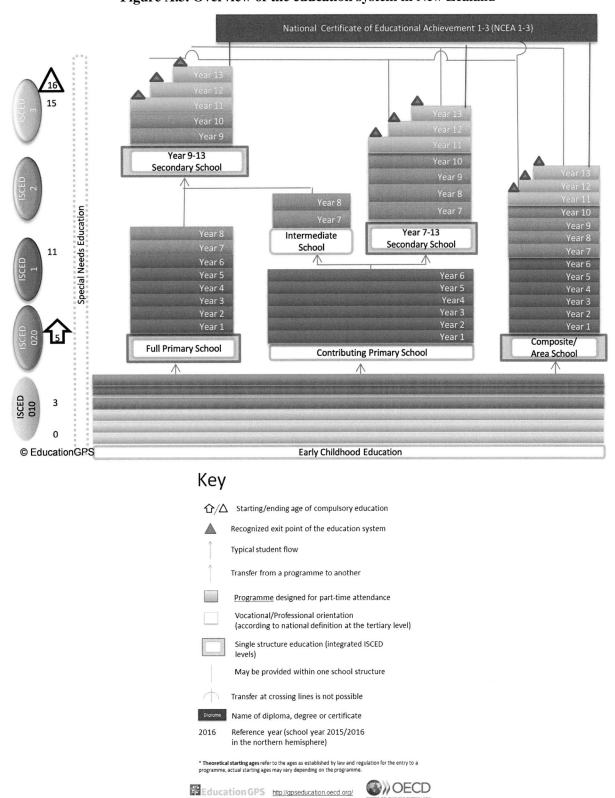

Source: OECD (2016), "Overview of the education system in New Zealand", OECD Education GPS, http://gpseducation.oecd.org/Content/MapOfEducationSystem/NZL/NZL_2011_EN.pdf.

References

Ministry of Education (n.d.), "New Zealand Education System: Overview", Ministry of Education, Wellington, www.education.govt.nz/assets/Uploads/NZ-Education-System-Overview-publication-web-format.pdf.

Ministry of Education (2017), "New Zealand School System", www.newzealand now.govt.nz/living-in-nz/education/school-system.

OECD (2016), "New Zealand: Overview of the education system", OECD Education GPS, http://gpseducation.oecd.org/CountryProfile?primaryCountry=NZL&treshold=10&topic=EO.

OECD (2013), *Education Policy Outlook: New Zealand*, OECD Publishing, Paris, www.oecd.org/education/EDUCATION%20POLICY%20OUTLOOK%20NEW%20ZEALAND_EN.pdf.

Immigration New Zealand (2016), "The school system, Immigration New Zealand", Wellington, www.newzealandnow.govt.nz/living-in-nz/education/school-system.

New Zealand Parliamentary Library (2004), "Schools Funding: An introduction", Parliamentary Library, Wellington, www.parliament.nz/resource/mi-nz/00PLSoc RP04051/3b464c6bf055f552afa1a14ccab498b196256778.

Annex B

Representatives on education for Indigenous students in participating jurisdictions

Country	Province/Territory/State	Contacts
Canada	Alberta	Karen Andrews Marisa Cooper Janusz Zieminski
	Manitoba	Dino Altieri Tia Cumming Rhonda Shaw Jeden Tolentino
	New Brunswick	Monica Le Blanc John McLaughlin Kim Skilliter
	Northwest Territories	Angela James Jessica Schmidt John Stewart
	Nova Scotia	Sarah Curry Shannon Le Blanc Wyatt White
	Yukon	Simon Blakesley Ashraf Mahmoud
New Zealand		Charlotte Harris-Miller Steve May Māhina Melbourne David Scott
Australia	Queensland	Selwyn Button Christopher Kinsella John Tracey Susan Vesperman Claudia Whitton

ORGANISATION FOR ECONOMIC CO-OPERATION AND DEVELOPMENT

The OECD is a unique forum where governments work together to address the economic, social and environmental challenges of globalisation. The OECD is also at the forefront of efforts to understand and to help governments respond to new developments and concerns, such as corporate governance, the information economy and the challenges of an ageing population. The Organisation provides a setting where governments can compare policy experiences, seek answers to common problems, identify good practice and work to co-ordinate domestic and international policies.

The OECD member countries are: Australia, Austria, Belgium, Canada, Chile, the Czech Republic, Denmark, Estonia, Finland, France, Germany, Greece, Hungary, Iceland, Ireland, Israel, Italy, Japan, Korea, Latvia, Luxembourg, Mexico, the Netherlands, New Zealand, Norway, Poland, Portugal, the Slovak Republic, Slovenia, Spain, Sweden, Switzerland, Turkey, the United Kingdom and the United States. The European Union takes part in the work of the OECD.

OECD Publishing disseminates widely the results of the Organisation's statistics gathering and research on economic, social and environmental issues, as well as the conventions, guidelines and standards agreed by its members.

OECD PUBLISHING, 2, rue André-Pascal, 75775 PARIS CEDEX 16
(91 2017 09 1 P) ISBN 978-92-64-27941-4 – 2017